SPRINKLES FROM HEAVEN

Stories of Serendipity

Nonfiction / Inspirational / Spirituality

www.CarolynJaynes.com
SprinklesfromHeaven@gmail.com

Cover Design by Natalie Walstein
www.LovelyLettersPress.com

Art Concept by Stefan Talian and Carolyn Jaynes
www.StefanTalian.com

Photography by Rich Sjoberg & Geoff Martin

Professionally Edited by Dave Feldman

Published by Passion & Faith Press
San Diego, California
PassionandFaithPress@gmail.com

ISBN: 978-0-9914776-0-9 Softcover 4/23/15 4th Printing
ISBN: 978-0-9914776-1-6 E-book

San Diego, California

WITH DEEP GRATITUDE

Thank you God, angels, my spirit guides, my deceased beloved ancestors, and fully alive loved ones.

Thank you to my cousin Rich Sjoberg for assisting with my relocation to San Diego, and always being there when I needed help. I am grateful to my *soul sister* cousin Cheryl Felling who always believed in me as a writer.

Thank you Mom, Janet Carmichiel, for being the unconditionally loving, supportive rock in my life and for her gentle husband Jim, the best stepdad a woman could have.

Thank you Dad for telling me I could be whatever I put my mind to. I believed you.

Thank you to my Grandmother, LaVerne Smith, who showed me women could be high achievers.

My great Grandmother, Agnes Baarsen, told me if I wanted to be a writer I should read everything I could get my hands on. I did.

HEARTFELT THANKS

Many thanks to the Wesley Palms Writer's Critique Group—these editors, professional writers, and supportive mentors made this book a reality. I am grateful for the countless earth angels who contributed innumerable ideas and supported my creative process. I didn't know it would take a village to write a book. It does. I send my love to all who made a difference. You know who you are.

I gratefully acknowledge all paths to God. I honor all brave souls and spiritual pioneers who dare to fly free and be your deepest, most creative self.

I take no position on any outside issues. This is only my experience. All of these stories are true, although some names may have been changed for confidentiality.

I thank you, the precious soul who holds this book, for reading me. I hope it inspires you to manifest your own miracles and serendipity, share your spiritual gifts, and be the brightest light you can be to bring hope to our universe. Follow your bliss with passion and faith . . .

Table of Contents

Table of Contents

Table of Contents

I dedicate this book to my beloved adult children, Jeremy and Natalie, who let me go—to live my dreams in San Diego, California. I love you deeply.

SERENDIPITY STRIKES AGAIN

"Look out!"

Skating backwards, I released my male skate partner and quickly spun around to see what the commotion was about. A waltzing couple had stopped roller-skating right behind us. The warning made me quick-stop, avoiding a messy collision. The skinny blond man with the big voice was off to the side of the roller rink, smiling like The Good Samaritan.

"Whew! Thank you," I said, rolling over to him. "Hi, my name is Carolyn. You must be an angel." I reached for his hand in gratitude.

"I'm Greg. Call me Road Angel. That's my nickname," he said, still grinning.

I chuckled, "Well, that's appropriate."

My partner sped off to the now faster music and I talked with my new friend who saved me. I thought he was interesting, so I invited him over for a homemade dinner the next night.

* * *

When Road Angel came to my condo, he saw my

Bible on the top shelf of my bookcase, an old holiday gift from my sly Grandma Vernie.

Road Angel opened it, then looked at me curiously. “Have you read it?” he teased.

It did look dusty. “No, just the red-inked quotes from Jesus. The rest of it turned me off with all that violence and patriarchal dogma they try to shove down my feminist throat.”

“That is not the way of Jesus,” Road Angel said, looking concerned. “You could keep reading more. Maybe your bias is just a way to stay estranged from the church.”

Estranged? Not even acquainted. I was never properly introduced. I thought religion was for simpletons and widows. I was raised without spiritual guidance from my parents. My dad wanted me to make up my own mind about church when I grew up. Even as an adult in my 40’s, religious rituals were foreign to me. My mom was quasi-Lutheran. Her mother, Vernie, a professional pianist, played her church’s organ, and sometimes took my mom with her. But luckily my parents took me to the roller rink on Sundays, instead of church. Road Angel disclosed at the rink that he attended a weekly Bible study group. I was surely a novice compared to him. I didn’t know where to begin. "So, where should I start reading?"

"Start with Matthew."

* * *

I read it the next night. It was about Jesus healing the sick, talking in parables, and salt-of-the-earth stuff. As I was reading my Bible, my former next-door neighbor, Linda, called me, wanting to reconnect. We hadn't spoken since I moved away from our townhouse complex over a year ago. Not a close friend, she kindly gave her teen daughters' hand-me-downs to my daughter, Natalie, and we cat-sat for each other. All I knew about her was that she seemed religious from the Christian crosses I saw on her walls.

After we caught up a bit, Linda asked, "Would you like to go to my church with me?"

Linda had never invited me out before. *Why now and why church?* Then an eerie feeling rose up in me as I recalled an old, dark, probably haunted brick church near my childhood home on the corner of Pleasant Avenue in Minneapolis. It had always given me the creeps. But her invitation was so timely, I had to consider it.

"We could sing together," she said to persuade me.

I resisted. "I doubt if I would know anything you

sing at church." I felt less than secure, quite unreligious, and more estranged from the church than Road Angel could ever imagine.

"You never know. Just come along."

* * *

So I went. Linda picked me up in her tidy sedan. I'd forgotten how wholesome she looked; she was a slim brunette, perky and petite. On the way we saw two bumper stickers that seemed to know where we were headed, "Met Jesus?" and "Honk if you know Jesus." I was also reading a book at home on meaningful coincidences, also known as synchronicity or serendipity, when these weird signs began to show up.

Grace Church was massive, almost intimidating, with hundreds of people filing into the pews. I sensed a lot of anticipatory energy, yet I felt out of place. I wouldn't know anyone, except Linda, and she was singing in the choir on stage before she sat next to me. I wouldn't know any of her churchy songs.

We were early so we went into the church bookstore and I saw a big book there titled *Amazing Grace*. It stood out from all the hundreds of other spiritual books in the little shop.

"Oh look, Linda. That's the song I sang at my Grandma's funeral. Her name was Grace. I love that song."

Linda looked up at me and nodded. Then she left to change into her choir robe. I took my seat with the congregation near the back, feeling alone, out of place, and conspicuous. *What the hell am I doing here? Don't cuss, Carolyn, you're in church!*

Randomly, I opened the Bible from the shelf in front of me. I began reading on the exact same page that I had been reading at home, the now familiar Book of Matthew and the Beatitudes. *Hey, what a coincidence. I'll tell Road Angel about this.*

The choir sang with a fervor. Afterwards, Linda sat next to me on the bench. I still felt uneasy, even though the pews were padded and the parishioners closest to me had just welcomed me. Next a large video screen flashed on and the lyrics lit up as I recognized the first line to the *one* gospel song I knew, *Amazing Grace.*

I stood there astonished. "Really? 'Amazing Grace?' We're singing that? Oh, cool."

Linda turned to me, "God sure is trying to get your attention."

Together we sang *Amazing Grace.* It was a soothing, bonding bridge between us. I felt so comforted by the inspirational lyrics and familiar melody. It felt like coming home.

"We haven't sung that one in months." Linda said, smiling.

I nodded. Some strange serendipity had somehow struck. Next we were asked to open our Bibles. It was again the same page I had opened earlier.

"Wow. This is too weird," I said. "That's what I was reading at home."

Linda grinned like she understood. Her eyes twinkled with light.

The grand finale was at the end of the pastor's uplifting sermon. "The Christian doctrine actually contributed to women's rights," the pastor explained from the pulpit. "No other religion gives as much value to women."

True or not, it hit me where I lived.

Had God been watching my every move? Hearing my every thought?

All my objections were addressed and overcome as if the preacher could read my contrarian mind. I turned to

Linda, threw up my hands in surrender and said, "Serendipity strikes again."

THE HUMMINGBIRD

Do you have a special sign from God? A sign that you know is personally meant just for you? I do. It might be finding a perfect feather on my path that tells me everything will be all right. Or the appearance of a shiny coin to let me know I don't have to worry about money. Best of all, it's a hummingbird that shows up when I'm having difficulties in my life—when I need a spiritual lift and reassurance of God's love for me. For some Native Americans, it means good luck, hope, and joy.

I had serious financial challenges. I had just broken up with my boyfriend, Michael. Then when I suspected my supervisor was stealing, I told the company boss. Instead of investigating my claim and getting rid of him, they got rid of me! Not only was I grieving the loss of my sweetheart, now I was also out of work and money.

To pay the rent, I needed income quickly, so I took the first job offer that came along—a garden center sales job I'd done twenty years before. I was frustrated and frazzled with the complex computer system. I'd been trained as a therapist and I wanted a counseling career and this busy retail position was not it.

After a month of low-paying manual labor, my back hurt, my feet ached. I felt downhearted, trapped, and exhausted from the toil. Dreading another tough day, I trudged off to work. I walked along the sidewalk, head down, toward the parking lot, when a radiant hummingbird appeared on my path. It fluttered directly in front of me, flying at eye level to get my attention—dancing magically on the wind. I admired its incredible beauty.

"Hello, aren't you beautiful."

In response to my remark, it flitted up, down, and spun around, flaunting its glorious neon green back. I felt all light and giddy inside, like a delighted child, so amused by this funny creature as it swirled in circles to entertain me. My little performer made me belly laugh. It was such a stark contrast, I knew then I had to leave that crummy job to be happy.

Because that lovely hummingbird inspired me with jubilation, I went in that very day and quit my job *in full faith*. My sign from the hummingbird let me know I was going to be all right, and I was. Within a week I had an exciting new job offer at a counseling center that paid better and more importantly, I loved it.

BOB'S HOPE

I somehow knew that I needed to see Bob that day to say goodbye. The terminal diagnosis of cancer had been cast two years earlier, but the reality of his death sentence sank in starkly when I saw Bob the last week of his life. Our relationship had ended before the birth of our son, Jeremy, aged nineteen. I was grateful that Jeremy had time to live with his Dad, because Bob, only forty-two years old, would soon be gone. Bob, Jeremy, and his two step brothers had won a "Make a Wish" grant to vacation at Disneyland, but he wouldn't be alive long enough to make the trip.

I entered the dimly lit living room-turned-hospice and was surprised to see Bob, attached to an oxygen tank, sitting up in his chair, complaining that his feet hurt. I had been told that his swollen feet were a sign that his organs were shutting down. He tried to pop the tab on his Pepsi can. I reached forward to help him, but he insisted he could do it himself. He couldn't. When I offered again, he scolded me.

"If you keep asking me that, you will have to leave,"

he snapped, not wanting to admit that this simple task was getting the best of him. I overlooked his grouchy mood, thinking I might be grumpy too if I were about to die. Being that weak and helpless must feel awful to a man once so strong and independent, who was now about to leave everyone and everything behind to the living. I sat quietly and smiled at him, unsure what to say next. I felt awkward since we hadn't talked very much in years.

"I assume you are here because you *care,*" he said.

"Yes," I nodded. "How are you feeling?"

"I'm so tired," he groaned.

His cancer that started in his esophagus had spread to his back and stomach. He had control of his intravenous morphine pump to medicate his pain, and I saw him thumb the button for a dose.

I wanted to talk to him about God and discuss the practical matter of our son and his two teenaged stepsons he had sole custody of. I managed a sentence or two about how I believed he had guardian angels to assist him to the afterlife, but he didn't seem to accept the nearness of his impending death, or if he did, he wasn't going to discuss it with me.

I felt sad to see him so sick and hurting. He had

been stocky, and now that he had stopped eating he looked like a tiny bag of bones. I reached out to hug him farewell.

Bob blurted out in fear, “Don’t squeeze me!”

“I’m not going to squeeze you, I promise.” I kissed his sunken cheek softly and patted the other one lightly. Then I whispered, “Goodbye, Bob.”

He replied confidently, “See you later.”

I turned to leave the house, knowing it was the last time I would see him alive. As I drove home, my hand swiped the tears from my cheeks like a wet windshield wiper. Seeing him so close to death really upset me. I couldn’t stand to see him like that.

Bob died a couple of days later at home, the way he wanted to die.

The next day I was on the phone with my friend Susan in Arizona when my computer went crazy. I felt Bob’s presence in the room. I was receiving instant messages on my monitor as if I were online. My name kept flashing urgently in a text box across the screen to get my attention. *This can’t be*, I told myself, yet it was happening.

“I feel like Bob is trying to contact me through the computer,” I told Susan, who is spiritually aware and believed me. The computer was making black vertical lines, something I didn't even know how to do, and had never seen before, or since. If that wasn't enough, the words on the screen turned red without my clicking the color icon. I hadn't touched anything.

I was astonished, then I felt relieved that Bob was all right, even honored that he chose to come to me in spirit. He must have known that I would welcome him. The hairs on my arms raised up as a shivery wave went through my body. Just as suddenly as he came, he quickly left, apparently satisfied he had made the connection.

A few days later I had a vivid dream. Bob stood tall and strong, healthy and vibrant once more. He held out his arms wide as if to hug me and said with a big grin, "You can squeeze me now!"

I was delighted to see that he was happy and I had no reason to be worried any longer. I awoke with the feeling that this was not a typical dream. It felt real. It appeared that Bob wanted to give me this gift, the reassurance that he was out of pain. I didn't have to be sad about his death anymore because he looked joyful and free. I rolled over in my warm bed, smiling with hope that he will, like he said, see me later.

A PRECOGNITIVE DREAM

The night before I flew solo to Jamaica I had a dream that my luggage was inspected by airport security personnel. I felt scared in the dream even though I had nothing to hide. I also dreamt I was wearing a strange maroon outfit, not a color I typically wear, and I saw a rowboat nearby on a sandy shore. This dream was a strong warning to me to avoid some kind of danger. It had a foreboding feel to it. The maroon color stuck in my mind most of all.

The next day I was at the Minneapolis airport, excited for my first excursion abroad. The long passenger line was tolerable and then security picked me out of the line-up and asked to search my bags. This normally would have frightened me, but because of my dream, I readily handed over my suitcases. I was relieved of anxiety, however illogical, since I half expected it.

"It's routine," the inspector stated, "We randomly choose bags to search."

I was chosen this time. Still, it felt awkward to be searched like a suspected criminal.

* * *

A few days into my Jamaica trip, I was exploring the enchanting tropical beach of Montego Bay and noticed I had lost my expensive prescription sunglasses in the sand. I was upset because I had never spent so much money for fashion eyewear before, and now they were gone. About this time I also met a pudgy, middle-aged Jamaican security guard at the seaside resort where I stayed.

"Do you need anything?" he asked me, smiling at me as we walked along the beach.

"I was looking for my sunglasses, but I've given up," I said sadly.

Then I watched that man scan the shoreline for the next several hours. I was having dinner when he came up to me and showed me my sunglasses he had hunted for all day. I was ecstatic!

"Wow. Thank you. I can't believe you found them." I smiled as he handed them to me.

He looked like a prideful cat with a prize bird or a tasty mouse to offer me. I handed him a twenty-dollar bill in gratitude. He gladly took it.

"Do you want to go dancing with me tonight?" he

asked with a flirt in his eye.

"No." I saw a wedding ring on his fat finger and he wasn't my type even if he'd been single. He kept hanging around me, uninvited. So I left to get ice water to dissuade him.

* * *

Later that evening I was reading by the shore in the dimming evening light when he came over and sat too close to me on a double lounger. He talked about his wife and four children.

"I would divorce her if you would marry me," he lied. "Sell all your assets in America and come live with me on the island." He put his groping hand on my arm.

The next thing I knew he was kissing me hard and grabbing my hand to lead me to my first-floor hotel room. This so-called security guard, who had so kindly retrieved my sunglasses, now appeared to think I owed him more than money.

Just then I saw the face of a ghastly monster superimposed on his human face. My inner alarm went off and I was filled with foreboding, like a strong spiritual warning.

I looked down at what I was wearing—my maroon

jumpsuit! Déjà vu swept through me. Then I saw the rowboat next to the palm tree off to the side of my lounge chair, just like my dream. Frightened, I quickly pulled my hand away from his, bid him goodnight firmly, and ran off to my hotel room as fast as I could, bolting the door behind me. With my heart pounding, safe in my room, I dropped onto the bed, exhaled in relief, grateful for the warning. I thanked God for my protection from this unruly brute.

After I settled down, I felt alone and vulnerable. Then I prayed for my soul mate to come into my life.

THE COSMIC CONNECTION

On a lovely March evening, while e-mailing friends on my computer, an instant message suddenly grabbed my attention by declaring, "Mark has sent you an instant message—will you accept?" I had been receiving many inquiries to my "Wild Windsurfing Woman" singles ad online, but this one came from outside the confines of America Online. It had a more mysterious, other-world quality to it than the little chat-box interruptions that usually appeared on my computer screen.

I accepted his invitation and we began a lively chat. "Boo!" was Mark's way of saying hello. We bantered back and forth and made each other laugh, him with his written "giggle" and me with my smiley face and LOL for *laughing out loud,* which his messages had a way of instigating. We clicked online and it was fun reading his quips, counteracting with my own spunky comebacks, and my heart fluttered with each flirt.

Mark and I began to sense a growing camaraderie unlike other cyber chats. We are both writers, teachers, and work helping others. We each had a strong belief in God.

The humor and innate understanding between us was so refreshing.

We wanted to meet in person after only a few, long written interactions. Excitement and anticipation engulfed me, unlike my previous blind dates. He would sweetly call me by name on the computer screen and I sensed his passion and tenderness, a preface to something profoundly personal that he was about to reveal to me, as I read my own name "Carolyn…" It was as if his voice was whispering to me from his pillow—his soul deep into mine.

I *felt* him in his words, and I was drawn to him.

He asked me to call him at work. In his online profile he had written his favorite quote, "The sun doesn't shine on the same dog's butt every day."

"What's that supposed to mean?"

He explained that not every day can be a fiesta. Then he described what his office looked like. I felt honored that in some sacred way he was describing himself, wanting me to know who he was. Even stranger, I felt like I already *knew.*

There was a basic trust building, so I took a risk and e-mailed him a story I had written while traveling to

Jamaica. I asked him to read it and return it with his impressions. I was offering him a part of my inner being, as my writing is an essential, integral part of me, and the vacation had been a spiritual transformation.

I attached this to an e-mail and sent it to his office:

Slowin' It Down in Jamaica

I got away from my hectic work life by jetting to Jamaica but it took some adjustment before I caught up to the slower pace. *Travelers must expect to wait*, I told myself. I am the most impatient person I know. Expect to wait, yes, but many tourists don't. They expect immigration to grant them special entitlement, for customs to wave them quickly through, and airport transportation to issue an immediate thumb's up. It was the waiting that initially helped me make a conscious decision to *relax*.

Behind me, a well-to-do lady was complaining how slow the airport official was. I had now accustomed myself to this new country, rather than expecting, like many Americans, to have the country bend to our rigid rules of expediency.

My itinerary paperwork was incomplete due to a

last-minute booking, so I didn't have a voucher for the shuttle bus to my hotel. I didn't panic. I trusted and remained calm, explained that it was my understanding that a ride was included in my tour package. I waited some more, inside the air-conditioned terminal, longing to get outside and feel the Caribbean sun on my white winter cheeks.

I was placed with a less-than-pleased van driver who probably wouldn't get reimbursed. I made an effort to be especially friendly, tipped him well, and left his vehicle with the card he gave me, offering to be my personal escort during my stay. From the smile in his eyes, I knew that driving wasn't all he was offering me. Flattered, I respectfully left his taxi. *Welcome to Jamaica!*

I entered the open courtyard to the Montego Bay Inn. Impressed and utterly delighted, I was greeted by dazzling tropical plant life, mirrored by a turquoise swimming pool and an amazing ocean horizon. I was struck by the majestic beauty surrounding me, singing birds, and sweet floral scents on the warm breeze. I didn't let the fact that my reservation wasn't completed, and that the hotel was full, get me down.

So I waited.

These lessons in patience, tolerance, and remaining serene under stress were building up my virtues. It was hot in my long black pants as I lay blissfully in the incredible tropical sunshine on a white plastic lounge chair by the pool. The Jamaican hospitality never wavered for a moment. I was given fruit punch then a cold 7-Up, they called other hotels for me, and then my reservation was finally confirmed. I had arrived at twelve thirty a visitor, but by four o'clock I had guest status. I had spent the afternoon eyes closed, lying back, listening to popular American music from huge speakers. In this beautiful place I just knew everything would be all right.

My room had two double beds with brightly colored bedspreads, off-white ceramic floors, and white wicker furniture with thick floral printed cushions. Decoratively speaking, I had gone from January in Minnesota to a Jamaican July.

Pleased with my place, I took a refreshing shower and settled in, and laid out my minimal possessions on the other bed. I was starving after only eating breakfast on the plane at seven thirty a.m. I ordered a BLT sandwich at the outdoor grill, facing the ocean. Even though it had mayo, it was the best BLT I've ever had.

I checked out the shore of the beach, amused by baby crabs running for cover under craggy rocks, dodging the rushing water and me, a weary American transplant in cultural and climate assimilation mode. I had gone from a frosty dark morning in a freezing car, with ice crunching under my tennis shoes, shivering under the Airport Bus Depot's heat lamp that wasn't doing its job. After a mere four hour plane trip, I was absorbing intense light and divine heat, lush green foliage, pink hibiscus, teal waters, and friendly native people adorned with bright-colored clothing and white smiles. Even though they were all working and busy, their luminescent eyes were full of contentment. I wanted some of that.

I shed my bikini cover-up and eagerly plopped into the ocean barefoot, happily squeezing gray muck up between my impoverished toes. I went for a heavenly swim, tentatively wondering if jellyfish and stingrays like the warm shallows. The water was as luxurious as a bath. I crawled along the bottom until my hand brushed against something that felt like a porcupine. I backed up, suddenly aware of my ocean naiveté and headed back to shore to safely collect shells imbedded in rock crevices.

The clean ocean air, the backdrop of reggae music,

and the scent of the open grill were all pleasures to my awakening senses. The sun was setting shortly before five thirty, so I took a nap, nude in the air conditioned hotel room. I awoke at seven p.m., precisely as the dinner buffet was commencing. The outdoor spread offered beef soup, rice with green peas, and Jamaican jerk pork—a delectable island entrée. My eyes lit up over ripe red tomatoes, cantaloupe, watermelon, and fresh pineapple—a gorgeous display of fresh fruits I hadn't eaten since last summer.

When traveling solo, it has always been dining alone that has made me feel the most conspicuous. In this family atmosphere, I seated myself with a group of people at a very large table, as if I were part of their family. Just as I felt secure blending in, they all got up and left me there, and I was self-consciously all alone at a very large table. A live reggae band with a xylophone played, hopelessly trying to rouse the hundred or so overfed, sluggish tourists.

I was dreamily star-gazing, thrilled at how bright the sky was, and glad the moon was full. My spirit wanted to dance but my jet-lagged body knew it would have to be another night. My sun-burnt eyes were fighting my contact lenses and I wanted to wake up early to see the glorious sun. As a tribute to the timelessness of this paradise island, my watch stopped. I asked a waiter what time it was.

He looked at his watch. "8:58."

"Oh," I said, "it's nine o'clock."

"No," he corrected me gently, "Two minutes before nine."

He was right. I would have cheated myself out of two full minutes. Each moment matters here. I like it—it's the happiest way to be.

Back at my hotel room, music infiltrated the windows which were more like wooden shutters that you can easily open and close. There were no screens, no bugs, only a clean breeze. Some merchants had spread their wares on blankets across the dining lawn, so I bought my daughter Natalie a five-dollar beaded bracelet, not wanting to dicker on the price, only to have it work its way out of my pocket from the beach to my room. Nothing, however, could steal my joy from being here.

I love Jamaica and I think Jamaica loves me too.

Foreign travel stretches me—questions my lifestyle, challenges my views. I'm convinced that the Midwest is home to people who don't like to venture out much.

I was propositioned three times by adoring Jamaican security guards, to keep me company in my hotel room.

Who, I joked, is going to protect me from *them*? They give new meaning to an *all-inclusive* resort. Before this trip was over, I even had two marriage proposals. I don't think it was me personally that won their hearts as much as it was my (assumed wealthy) American whiteness, my vacation status, my singlehood, and the fact that I was wildly windsurfing in my bikini for days by myself, which meant I was a woman who had to be tamed.

I was intrigued by the idea of shedding my former Minneapolis life and living on this incredible island, but I wasn't nuts about matrimony. My admirers settled for a Kodak moment together and a promise of sending them a photo to an address they scribbled on hotel napkins. Regretfully, I went back home to the winter fog, where I once again merged with the every-day people, who treated me like the ordinary person I forgot I was.

* * *

I was delighted when Mark's thoughtful response arrived in my e-mail box the next day.

Ah, Inspiration! by Mark

Inspiration is a wonderful rush…or, it is to me! And where has this "rush" come from? Is it the sunshine? The prospect of spring coming? My own spark of enthusiasm? Actually the inspiration is from a memoir from a little lady who took time to record some of her feelings and observations concerning a well-deserved vacation to Jamaica.

I will assume that her writing was for her a time of reflection, a time of soul scrubbing, that only another writer would understand.

Her prose weaved ever so lightly and calmly about her travel difficulties as they popped up, doing their best to dampen her optimism—but Murphy had met his match this time. Patience triumphed–*patiently*. And due to her spiritual balance, she enjoyed herself immensely by not only adapting to a different culture, but also amalgamating with her environment. I found only one "flaw" in her monograph. The last statement, more specifically, the last seven words:

"Regretfully, I went home to the winter fog where I once again merged with the everyday people, who treated me like *the ordinary person I forgot I was*."

These words were spoken after returning to her native Midwestern surroundings. On second thought, this is not a "flaw" but a notable example of humility and wisdom. As I personally have had the privilege to banter with this insightful lady, and in less than twenty four hours will be graced by her presence.

Every word ever written has a different "flavor" depending on who takes the time to read it and listen to its voice. When this lady wrote about her trip, did she give thought to the flavor I am about to share back with her? In her humility, I think not.

After being married for eighteen years, and deciding that I could no longer wear a "mask" of happiness, I am separated and on the painful road to divorce. So maybe I am a little more sensitive to feelings, both my own and others. On the surface, it seems like a stretch between one person's vacation reflections and another's emotional reconstruction, but to me, at this juncture in life, it's a catwalk.

This lady and I have invested some of our precious time in each other. Listening, giggling, blushing, and just "chatting," all the time forming a cognitive image of each other. Then after many attempts, our photographs were exchanged and our feelings toward each other remained unchanged, as we already liked what we "saw" by way of our hearts. But you still don't see the connection between the two stories . . .

Well, here it is, as I see it. Like her journey from the cold winter tundra to a warm tropical paradise, I find myself journeying from the "cold" winter of a dead relationship to a possible warmer, inviting friendship. Her journey was so rewarding because she was patient, adapting to a slower pace, and blending with the culture. Not giving up who she was, as much as combining the two together to form a unique alloy. And this is what she has encouraged me to do on this eve of our meeting in person; slow down, be patient, and see if we have a "connection" or as I would term it, do we "click" in the paradise of relationships? The thought of paradise inspires me and with her as my guide, I'm sure things will work out for the best whatever the final destination. – *Mark*

* * *

He wrote beautifully and intelligently, in a way that made it clear he was a man who understood what I had gone through—a man who understood me for the first time in my life. He also pointed out the same "flaw" that my mother had pointed out. It was about my being "ordinary." My mother, of course, doesn't see me that way. Neither did Mark. He protested the same line, yet got what I meant. I was so intimately touched, I wept in front of my computer screen.

Mark had written in his prose, "We liked what we saw by way of our hearts." I couldn't have said it more succinctly. It was true, as my friend Nancy so accurately described cyber-dating, as "meeting someone from the inside out." I felt such joy making this connection that I felt a rush throughout my whole body. I loved him from his writing, before I even saw his picture, before we even met.

My perceptive ten-year old daughter, Natalie, who was coloring in a picture book next to me, suddenly looked up, pointed at my head and exclaimed, "Mom, there are lights shooting up from the top of your head. You look excited!"

"I am. You mean you see my aura? Draw it for me." Natalie drew tall lightning bolts rising vertically from my cartoon head on her scratch paper. It was true. I felt like I had made an internet connection with my soul mate, and my entire being was *delighted*.

Later that night, Natalie and I went to the video store and the movie that got my attention there was "You've Got Mail." I rented it, which in itself isn't that significant since meeting on e-mail was definitely on my mind, but later when I talked with Mark, he told me he had bought the "You've Got Mail" music soundtrack that same afternoon.

That night before bed I humbly collapsed to my knees in prayer, sobbing in gratitude to a God who had answered my prayers for my soul mate, and I begged to be worthy of such a gift.

We set up our meeting for Sunday at 1:30 pm. I could hardly wait. In New Age style, I consulted the dictionary for my "word of the day" divinity ritual, asking the Powers-That-Be:

"Where will I meet my soul mate?" With eyes closed, I flipped through the pages like shuffling cards, and the word that my finger randomly pointed to was "landing." I thought, OK, I travel, so maybe it will be at the airport?

Later Mark and I agreed to meet at his work-place—a modern marble building that was easy to spot. He described the lobby and said he would meet me at the bottom of the stairs, or the "landing." I felt the shiver of déjà vu spring up my spine. This meeting was going to be exceptional and I was sure of it. Somehow, it felt bigger than life, magical, surreal.

At this point I knew something profound was happening. I consulted The I-Ching Book of Changes, my Chinese fortune-telling book for a clue of what was to come.

"What is the nature of my relationship with Mark?" I asked The I-Ching.

I tossed the divinity coins three times to create a meaningful trigram. It read: "This, my fortunate friend, is a most auspicious sign. Among friends, this is the sign of blood brothers. Among lovers, this is the sign of soul mates. For all concerned, this is a good and true relationship, one with a strong male influence."

I was elated and a little scared. I decided to check it again, so I did a full I-Ching reading this time, with six coin tosses and came up with my hexagram description: I didn't need to look it up, I knew it by heart. I knew the sign for Heaven and there were two of them.

It was the best possible combination you can get for a compatible love relationship. Over the years I have done hundreds of I-Ching readings for myself and numerous friends and acquaintances for the entertainment value, and although much of it was highly accurate, I had never encountered this double yang symbol for anyone's relationship—not once!

My spirit soared as I became increasingly anxious.

Here is what the I-Ching said: "The Universe. Heaven over heaven. Sky beyond sky. Stars upon Stars. Whatever else it is, it will be big, huge, enormous, and everlasting. This is something that will change you forever . . . and for the good. A relationship achieves its full potential. The time for the BIG EVENT comes soon. In a word, the outcome is *cosmic*."

Wow. I felt my heart flutter. As a devoted believer in the power and wisdom of the I-Ching (which scares some people,) I was absolutely awestruck! How do I explain this to anyone? *No one will believe me.* I can hardly comprehend it myself. I have a lot of faith in God. My prayers have been coming true ever since I left my last relationship and vowed to be more spiritual. What's more, I had prayed to meet my soul mate. And now a couple weeks later I had the overwhelming sense that my true love and I were going to be reunited in this life.

The meeting was set for 1:30 so I went about my usual roller-skating routine that Sunday morning at The Roller Garden. At the risk of sounding corny, I told my friend, Old Man Morty, that I was going to meet my soul mate that afternoon.

He told me: “Your eyes are sparkling and there’s an illuminating new glow about you.”

I called my mother the night before and left my prediction on her voice mail, “Mom, I’m going to meet my soul mate tomorrow!” I had to tell someone, I was so jubilant.

I felt our profound connection in his writing, in his manly voice on the phone, the way he enunciated and emphasized his words, his innate understanding and very tender treatment of me. Something was definitely up. It felt out of this world.

I was much more down to earth and concerned about practical matters on the morning of our first date. *What does one wear to meet their soul mate?* I mused. My heart was racing, doing back-flips, like it had wings. I was filled with anticipation as I drove to the modern office building in Bloomington, Minnesota. I was already totally convinced I was in love with this wonderful new man and I hadn’t even met him yet.

Prior to this, I had checked on our astrological compatibility since I’m an amateur astrologer. We are both

Aries and his Moon was in Aries too, with both of us having the planet Venus in Aries—the planet of love, of course, which means we fall in love fast. Yup. Every combination and correlation seemed to point to ideal compatibility, harmony, partnership, and again, the words, "soul mates." I didn't reveal that I knew any of this when we met, and I tried to stay calm, but the butterflies in my stomach betrayed me.

I looked up from the landing of the elegant marble staircase and saw Mark standing there radiant and gorgeous, waving to me from the upper level. I should have paid more attention to this early unequal footing. It foreshadowed our overpowering connection from beginning to end. A more handsome man I have never met. He absolutely sizzled.

We smiled at each other. Grinning, he silently held out his hand for me to follow him and instinctively, wordlessly, totally trusting, I climbed the stairs with him and let him lead me down an atrium hallway.

Mark beamed as he said, "You look like a movie star." He pointed to a hand-written paper sign with my screen name on it, *Wild Windsurfing Woman*, and arrows pointing to where I should sit. On the cushioned bench was another sign he had made just for me, "Please be seated."

I noticed a portable compact disk player beside me with his soft music playing for us. Suddenly, he was in front of me. We were embracing and he was kissing me. He lifted his hand above our heads, sprinkling glittery confetti stars all over us! Kissing passionately in public, we were alternately laughing euphorically like drunken teenagers, unaware of all the people staring at us. I sat on his lap like I'd known him all my life. I felt a deep and joyful comfort in his presence, a loving peace and comfort that I hadn't known before, or since.

From here we walked outside around the quiet lake holding hands, stopping to read the paper love poems he had taken the time to tack onto the posts along the paved path two hours earlier. I was so enamored by his efforts that I could hardly read the words. I was falling irresistibly in love with him. Until then I didn't believe in love at first sight, now I felt it and no one on earth could talk me out of it. We giggled, bantered, and skipped side by side holding hands like children on a sugar high, oblivious to everyone. No one else even existed.

On the move now, we hugged and kissed again, in front of amused onlookers on our walk, like a highly romantic movie, the only lovers in the world.

The chemistry between us was instantaneous, unmistakable, overpowering. The rapport was immediate. It began to rain softly and we ran undaunted, giggling arm in arm all the way back to the office building. We didn't want our date to end.

"Would you like to attend church with me this evening?" I asked him. I felt a strong need to praise God and to be with Mark as long as possible.

He looked apprehensive. "What church?" He asked, possibly afraid I would try to convert him to an astrology cult or some cannibalistic New Age Voodoo sect.

So when I said, "Grace Church" he gasped with incredulous relief. The Baptist Church I mentioned was one he knew well, the same denomination as his own home church. So Mark came with me to church and we swayed to contemporary music together, singing close to one another like we had to be touching every minute. We prayed together. Later that night we went out to eat sensuous Chinese food that we both loved. Both of us started to cry as we shared intimate secrets together and then nurtured one another in complete understanding. Empathizing, we felt each other's separate pain deeply and intuitively, as if we were already lovers.

It was unmistakable that Mark is one of my greatest eternal loves. There is no doubt in my mind. I saw him again and again after that. Mark said he hadn't felt that good in years. I was hoping for about thirty-five more.

* * *

The song Mark played for me on his portable CD player the day we met was touching. Here is a part of it:

Anyone At All **by Carole King**

Funny how I feel, more myself with you
Than anybody else that I ever knew
I hear it in your voice; see it in your face
You've become the memory I can't erase

You could have been anyone at all
A stranger falling out of the blue
I'm so glad it was you

It wasn't in the Plan, not that I could see
Suddenly a miracle came to me

Safe within your arms, I can say what's true
Nothing in the world I would keep from you
You could have been anyone at all
An old friend calling out of the blue
I'm so glad it was you . . .

* * *

There was just one little problem in all of this wonderful, blissful love between us. Mark was married. His "separated" status was really a couch in his office in the same home as his wife of eighteen years. At least that's what he told me since I was never over there. He also lived with his sixteen-year-old son and his daughter just out of high school. He asked his wife, Valerie, for a divorce two months before we met. She was taking it badly, begging him to stay. Her desperate pleas left him feeling guilty, indecisive, and immobilized.

I continued to see him despite his precarious marital status, believing in him when he said he was getting a divorce. I thought it might be weeks at first, then months. But when it wasn't happening I became disillusioned, angry, and torn over our illicit relationship, between what's right and wrong. I found myself in a situation I had avoided all my life—being involved with a married man.

I was in love with *this particular man,* and he just happened to be married to someone else. More than a mere red flag, this was a big bull-fighter's blanket, a huge deal breaker. It went against my values, yet I remained bull-headed about seeing him. I had to.

My bond to him was unmistakable, unavoidable, and to me, unbreakable. I was hopelessly smitten. Still boggled over how two strangers can fall in love so quickly, and completely, I registered for a class on past life regression to see if we had a past life connection. I hoped I could get some answers there, using hypnosis from a renowned and highly respected hypnotist and past life-regression therapist that a friend recommended to me in Minneapolis.

That day at class, at the urging of the master hypnotist's smooth and calming voice, I slipped into a deep trance. He had asked me to volunteer to be an example in front of the small class. He must've known I was highly susceptible to hypnosis because of my spiritual practices of prayer and meditation.

"Why are you here today?" he asked me.

"To find out if Mark and I have known each other before. I met my soul mate at the end of March and I want to know if we were in love in another life because our bond is so strong." I said matter-of-factly.

He asked, "Where do you feel his presence?"

I touched my swollen, vibrating heart, "here."

"What color is it?"

"Red."

He looked surprised. "Red denotes anger," he said.

I nodded yes. Of course I was angry. He hadn't left his wife for me.

Sensing my discomfort, he corrected himself. "It can also mean *courage*."

And yes, I felt I needed plenty of that. After this initial warm-up, the hypnotist put the whole class of eight people through a physical relaxation exercise and then a group meditation. When I was hypnotized again, he asked us to go back to a significant time when we lived before, long before we were born into this lifetime, to an era that addressed the question that we each came for.

"Notice how you are dressed. Look at your feet. What are you wearing?" he asked.

With my eyes closed, I looked down in my mind's eye as if in a dream-trance and saw a big clunky pair of men's brown boots on my feet. *Men's boots?* I was shocked.

"Follow that image up to your legs. What are you wearing?" he continued.

Dark trousers, sort of like Robin Hood would wear. I could see this like it was a movie screen behind my forehead—the images were colorful, clear, and quite real to me. I was re-living it. It was the essence of me, my spirit, inside a totally different body.

"Now go up further and see what you are wearing."

I was surprised to realize I was a large man. I sensed my bulging groin like a heavy package that hung in front of me. I could feel the surge of testosterone through my veins and I knew then why some males are so sexually motivated. It's not strong like that with most women.

I also knew I was in an old English countryside, standing in a lovely green meadow, next to a lone, mature oak tree. I was tall and stocky, a laborer of some sort, very muscular with broad shoulders—maybe a lumberjack.

I met my clandestine girlfriend (who is Mark now) under that tree as if it were our secret meeting place. She was stunning, an angel with long flowing blond hair reaching past her waist, dressed in a white flowing dress and a bewitching smile with eyes that glowed with love for me. My heart was instantly full, zapped by her intense devotion. I loved her very much and I knew she loved me. We were extremely happy together and I didn't want her to ever leave. She was my lover and my soul mate in that life.

I had gotten the answer I came for. I was sure of it now. Then the instructor asked what we were each experiencing in our individual meditations.

"I was a man in England during the Renaissance, in love with a beautiful blonde girl," I said.

He asked me to put myself into the place of that girl—to become her—and I was impressed that as a soul I was able to do this so easily. I moved my light into her body. I became *her*.

"The way you feel about the other, is that the way you feel about Mark?"

He was right on target. The abounding love energy was so real, so mighty, so unmistakably the same.

"Yes," I replied, amazed, as Mark's love for me in this life was confirmed, the same as mine for him. Our feelings for each other were equally intense and real.

"There you go."

And I *knew*. I was convinced beyond any doubt that the beautiful blonde woman was Mark's soul in this life and we knew each other before. Then, for what seemed like only five short minutes, I awoke from this hypnotic dream state to find that a full twenty-five minutes had passed in that enchanting place.

* * *

Later that night, I spoke with Mark on the phone, revealing our past life bond. "We've known each other before," I said softly.

"I know. . ." he whispered before he hung up.

The intensity of such an ecstatic reunion can only be surpassed by the agony of each inevitable separation. I shed so many tears that summer as I waffled back and forth over not wanting to hurt his family if they should discover our love affair, as well as the moral implications of what we were doing, and the fact that I wanted him so badly to be my husband. I wanted to be a person with high principles, to do God's will, and at the same time I wanted to hold Mark in my covetous arms. I was in a confusing, difficult dilemma.

I would tell Mark I wasn't going to see him until he was legally divorced, setting boundaries that I hoped would initiate his action, but two weeks later I would call him to come over. Or he would call or e-mail me. It was like we couldn't stay apart in spite of ourselves.

"Nothing can tear the two of you apart." The I-Ching reading rang true.

Everything I was ever taught came into question. I had once been so judgmental about women being involved with married men that it split up a close friendship I had. Now it was I who was "the other woman," the mistress in a secret love affair. To say the physical attraction was the strongest I have ever experienced is still an understatement. It felt more magical, more profound, so much more than sex. It was a cosmic connection.

I was immersed in his twinkling, loving brown eyes that he called his "stars," and consumed by the sensuous contours of his perfect face, and his deliciously wide, lopsided lips. A feeling of complete safety enveloped me. Intellectually, I should have been wary of meeting a stranger on the Internet. But this man was no stranger. He was my beloved. It was like something out of the Song of Solomon and an obscure book called, "Advice to a Young Wife from an Old Mistress." I read the following quote that confirmed and validated what I was going through:

"The strongest feeling I felt was *recognition,* as if I had known this man a very long time ago. Somewhere

Montaigne writes: 'We sought each other long before we met. We found ourselves so mutually taken with one another, so acquainted and so endeared betwixted ourselves, that hence forward nothing was ever so near to us as one another. Being begun so late, there was no time to lose.'"

This woman writer knew my situation.

I wanted to make sense of this. The only thing for sure was that it didn't make any sense. It was difficult to talk to anyone about it, because it was taboo, an extra-marital relationship. Even more than that, the spiritual quality of it was so out on the fringes of normalcy, who would believe me? I didn't know who to confide in. I did research into the study of soul mates, searching the Internet and library catalogs. There wasn't much there.

I found books on reincarnation, past life regression therapy, and reunited soul mates. After reading several books on these subjects, I found many threads and similarities that were too uncanny to be put aside as mere superstition. I discovered others who had experienced what I was now consumed by. I would never be the same.

My longing for him felt unbearable.

I cried pitifully. We weren't seeing each other,

because my friends and family insisted it was the right thing to do.

Now my tears rolled down with an aching heart. Mark said he would leave when his younger son graduated from high school, that it would be three years before we could be together.

Time slipped by and a week before Christmas I sent him this short e-mail message:

"I love you still and I always will." I couldn't help myself. I had to tell him.

He called three times that morning. We re-bonded instantly. He wanted to see me and I said no. I wanted him to leave his wife first.

He chided me, humorously, "I'm waiting for you to weaken."

"And I'm waiting for you to gather *strength*!"

We both laughed. We were at a stalemate. It was just a few more days before I realized how much I was giving up by not seeing him.

I had a disappointing date with a plain single guy I hardly felt anything for, who talked about wanting to have sex with me. The many climaxes Mark had given whenever we made love came to mind.

"No," I told him. "I only want to have sex with someone I love, who loves me." I called Mark at work to see if he would come over that evening. I couldn't settle for anything less now.

He was so thrilled and excited that he had difficulty interpreting the directions to my new house. He stammered over which road to take five times and still he got lost and was late.

As I waited for Mr. Bliss to arrive, the words of my practical, platonic friend Scott haunted me. He berated me, "Carolyn, it isn't *real*!"

But it felt real to me. I ran around in a frenzy lighting a dozen candles, putting on fresh makeup, making sure there was dinner to make. I even hid an aerosol can of silly string under the bed so I could spray him if he got too frisky. He once dumped all my neatly arranged shoes out of my closet like a naughty trickster. He was always being The Jokester, a rambunctious teenager in his forties, and I wanted to play my own little prank on him. My heart tangoed at the prospect of seeing him at my door. From a state of self-induced aloneness and romantic numbness, I suddenly came alive again.

He rang my bell.

There he was, my love of all loves, standing in my doorway, eyes a-sparkle, grinning from ear to ear, sheepishly telling me he was lost for half an hour.

"You look fabulous and your house is marvelous." He examined our new love nest.

I had fixed up the old dilapidated house and renovated it myself, feeling all the while I was creating a cozy home for *us*.

We fell into each other's arms again—so familiar and yet forgotten—how ecstatic it felt to touch each other again. By this time I had consoled myself. I was just going to love him, no matter what. I chose to feel secure, not doubt him, to respect his decision to stay with his family, even though it meant never being his one and only. I had come to a place of *acceptance* with him. During our separation I had faced all my fears, slaying the dragon of insecurity within, gaining composure to see it through, come what may.

I didn't realize it then, that all that waiting would be at my own expense.

As infuriated as I had been about his decision to not leave his home and family for me, I also admired the fact that he wanted to be a good father, that his family was important to him, that he had a sense of obligation to them. I implicitly understood his predicament—the fear of disruption, the financial chaos, the grief and loss of a family, albeit one that created little happiness for either spouse beyond routine. Still, I couldn't compete with that whole package, with all of them and a suburban house. It was just me, my cat, and a little refurbished bungalow.

Maybe this was our karma. Maybe I was the one who had stayed with my partner in that past life. Maybe this was a spiritual lesson on how it felt to be on the other end of it. How excruciating.

I had been through my own divorce in this life so I empathized with his avoidance of his break-up. I stayed longer than I wanted to with my ex-husband, Howard, because we had an adorable two-year old daughter together. An intact supportive family is something most of us want. I know I did.

It didn't help that Mark's wife was imploring him to stay, perhaps realizing what little leverage she had left, in a marriage predicated on her pregnancy. Their start was shrouded in secrecy, much like our affair. She told Mark she was on the pill even though she stopped taking it. Knowing the religion he was raised with, he felt obligated to marry her, and did so, with parental pressure. So Sarah was born and shortly after that, Jesse came. They all held him tightly in place. He couldn't let them down. He was the head of the household, their dutiful dad, their world.

I got his decision on November 1st, eight months after we met. His voice mail said, "I'm still hanging around." He said it in a depressing tone. "I'm going to hang around until Jesse leaves for college."

Mark said he had been defeated and crushed by his wife's desperate plea, "So why did we have Jesse then, if you were just going to leave us?" She cornered him. Mark said Jesse was sobbing too. "How could you just leave us like that? Who is going to take care of us, Dad?" His son's teary-eyed face left little to ponder. Mark stayed. He said he would stick around for three more years, just as his wife wished.

I was devastated.

I had been waiting anxiously for some kind of answer, but I really struggled over how he could really love me when he wasn't willing to leave. Was I just a pleasant distraction so he could tolerate his passionless marriage? A mere mistress to make love with?

Had he been lying to me the way he had been lying

to her about his whereabouts? Until then I had been so sure of him. Doubts crept in. No, they barged in. My denial crumbled. I saw his lies. He was cheating on her, and cheating me.

I felt like he had been dangling metaphorical carrots in front of me—a ravenous running jackrabbit I was, on an invisible racetrack going nowhere. I sent him my rage-filled retort in an impersonal e-mail, just as cowardly as his own voice mail message. Dramatically, I burned the black silk bathrobe I had given him for his birthday and watched it melt into nothingness—my unsuccessful attempt to extricate him from my soul—to unbind myself.

I wanted out of this agonizing attachment, to forget him. I recalled hearing the hypnotist share how he too had found his precious one-in-a-billion soul mate in this life and then she had committed suicide. I understood then why someone might feel like doing that.

I couldn't part with his love letters, his alluring photos. I hugged and buried my face in my unwashed pillowcases that smelled like him for months. *Eternity cologne, how appropriate! Eternal lust; then left in the dust.* I cried for a long time, over many weeks and months, whenever I thought about him, which was often.

Who can replace my soul mate? Who could there ever be after Mark?

I lost my resolve again. I saw him a few more times.

Whenever he left me he would always say, "I don't want to leave. Miss me, please."

My response would trail him like an echo as he walked out my door. "I already do . . ."

I finally stopped calling him, only to protect my heart. Since everyone who knew about him wanted me to stop seeing him, there was no one to share my intense grief with. I didn't do anything despairing, but I understood then why self-mutilating people cut themselves open. They want to see their pain on the outside, the oozing red blood, some visible confirmation of the dire emotion that can't express itself: Bloody validation. I stayed away from Mark and from sharp objects, and I wrote a poem that poured out of me.

THE MISTRESS

Like a widow whose beloved only comes to her in dreams
Like the lonely rock that holds on in the stormiest of streams
Heart ablaze with fire from some long-ago Great Spark
Shut out from his life, like a Secret in the dark
Hiding beneath the bumpy rug
Lest someone trip or fall
His family safe in their status quo
While I go through it all
Is love so hopeless a case as this?
Years of agony—for a few days of bliss?
Separations so long with each ecstasy sought
Love-sick misery is what fate brought
Waiting, always waiting for a move he never makes
Him, cozy on his fence
While my heart just swells, then breaks.

THE SILVER EARRING

To compensate for my aching heart, I bought myself a new pair of expensive silver earrings specifically for an upcoming singing performance. Then I went to the YMCA fitness center at ten o'clock in the morning to do my usual aerobic workout. When I emerged from the public shower, I saw that one of my pricey new purchases had disappeared from my earlobe. Aghast, I thought I just had to find it. I looked all over the floor, the shower stall, and the counters, but I couldn't find it anywhere.

Where on earth is it?

I asked God in a desperate prayer, "Please help me find my earring." Then I relaxed, knowing it would be taken care of. I thought about my friend Kathie who also had a YMCA membership and thought she might be going there later that day. So I called her.

"I lost one of my new silver earrings, Kathie. Will you please see if it's around anywhere when you go to the Y?"

"What does it look like?"

"It's silver and shaped like a teardrop."

Later that night after ten o'clock, I got a call from Kathie, who sounded excited. This was *twelve* hours after I'd lost my earring.

"I was leaving the front door of the YMCA when a woman I didn't know came running up behind me and asked me 'Is this your earring?'" Kathie said. "I couldn't believe my eyes. This lady was dangling your silver earring!"

FREEDOM FROM FEAR

I had an old black Kawasaki motorcycle that I loved to take on long speedy rides on the freeway. One dark afternoon it began to rain so hard that the pummeling threatened bodily harm. The droplets hurt as they impacted my body, even under my red leather jacket. I was far from home. Not only was I getting pelted and soaked, visibility was so poor that cars were stopped under the bridges to let the storm pass. The streets were full of water. I feared a flash flood. *One slide on the freeway and I could be killed.* Freezing, I didn't want to stop driving. I really wanted to get home. I was scared, so I asked God: "Please get me home safely."

Then I felt completely protected as if an invisible bubble surrounded me. I pulled into the shallowest wet lane, found a comfortable steady speed, and began humming and singing inside my helmet. The acoustics were good. I was serenading the little kid in me. My tension was gone, my fear had left, and I arrived home water-logged, but safe. I had put my life into the hands of my Higher Power and my faith freed me.

COMING OUT SIDEWAYS

In my Midwestern Norwegian family, anger was mostly suppressed. We were too nice. Therapists would probably call us "repressed." One wintry March day I was mad at my kids for being loud, playing rough, and not doing their chores—typical behavior for most children, especially ones who are housebound too long. I felt a storm brewing within me and although I didn't normally yell at my two kids, Jeremy, age twelve, and Natalie, only three, that day was different. We all had cabin fever and the air grew tense.

"Stop fooling around and finish your chores," I shouted. As I walked past the kitchen counter, some dirty dishes sitting there slid sideways and crashed loudly to the floor. They broke to smithereens. I hadn't touched them.

My kids saw it happen. They both stood still, deadly silent, eyes big, mouths open. I felt all fired-up with telekinetic power. Remember the movie *Carrie* and the fires she started with her eyes? It was kind of spooky like that, but without the flames. My face must have looked as surprised as theirs.

The kids got the message and got to work. Jeremy vacuumed while little Natalie emptied the small trash cans from the bedrooms.

I felt some kind of strange energetic release. I swept up the tiny bits of white glass plates off the kitchen floor into a dustpan. I was surprised that my anger had the power to move things. I didn't understand what had happened.

Did my aura bump them? How did my emotional energy—or energy-in-motion—come out sideways?

* * *

Another time, I was angry at my grandmother, Vernie, because I felt that she was mad at everybody in the house. She was cooking an elaborate holiday dinner at her crowded home for a dozen of us. She probably needed help, but she wasn't willing to ask for it or accept it. I was holding it all in again, as usual. So was she.

Suddenly, the ceramic casserole on the unlit stove-top burst and shot through the whole kitchen, burning and browning the linoleum floor. Everyone at the dining-room table screamed. It shocked everyone, except me. Instead, I felt a burst of emotional freedom from the shackles of my vested tension. Ah, relief. But everyone in the kitchen looked startled. I didn't want to be the one who caused all the commotion, but I felt like I was.

"I didn't do it," I blurted out. What I meant was I didn't *try* to do it.

My family looked at me strangely.

"Of course you didn't do it," my mom said, sweeping up the evidence of my energetic explosion.

Something inside me knew I had done it, that I had to do it, or I would have imploded.

There is so much more going on energetically, all around us, than we can see or hear.

* * *

One day as I was leaving my Jazzercise dance class, I focused on the coat hook that held my red winter jacket. I had the fleeting thought, *I want my coat*. I couldn't get to it with all the wet street shoes on the ground in front of it. As I thought that, my jacket instantly fell from its wall hook to the ground, like an obedient pet trying to come to me on command.

Ah, it heard me. I snickered.

If this can happen to me, it can happen to anybody. It's called *telekinesis*. Streetlights, video screens, and other electrical gadgets sometimes flash and flicker when I walk by or drive under them. I read that when we evolve spiritually, energetic instability can occur, causing electrical changes in our physical environment until we spiritually balance out on the next level.

I guess it's a sign that I'm evolving. I sure hope so.

BERNADETTE'S GOODBYE

Bernadette was going to die very soon, and I needed to persuade her family to put her on hospice care within our nursing home so she could get better care. As her Licensed Social Worker, it was my job to put that special service in place, delicately raise the issue with her traumatized family, and help my patient stay as comfortable as possible. But her family was in denial about her impending death.

In that day's emergency care conference, Bernadette's younger sister Annabelle talked about moving Bernadette into her family's home, unaware of the intense medical care it would entail. I knew, and all her nurses knew, it might be only be a matter of days, even hours, before Bernadette made her transition.

Her nurse told me quietly, "The smell of death is already in her room."

It took all day and a lot of gentle coaxing before the family finally put Bernadette, a curly blonde cancer patient in her fifties, on hospice care within the facility. I could see Bernadette's face turn ashen grey, and she became too weak in her wheelchair to push herself around. The soothing hospice nurse was there by her side now, monitoring her new pain medication.

Bernadette was running out of time.

"Can I get anything for you?" I asked, gazing into her weary slate-blue eyes. I put my hand on her crumpled knuckles that rested on her padded wheelchair arm-rails.

"I sure would like a 7-Up," she said meekly, "but I'm all out of change."

"I've got quarters." I dug into my blazer pocket. "I'll be right back." I walked out of her room. It was against hospital rules for staff to use our own money for any of the resident's needs, to lend or borrow anything, but who was going to know whether I was buying the soda for her or myself? Besides, it felt like a death wish, and that overrules.

I went to the first floor vending machine and bought her a cold can of 7-Up.

She looked so grateful when I handed her the soda and sat down next to her.

"Oh, thank you so much," she said, swallowing it slowly, savoring every sip.

"You're welcome," I said. "I wish I could do more."

But I couldn't do anything except sit with her. We sat together in silence until her clock chimed.

My day shift ended and I went home.

The same night that Bernadette was put on hospice care she died in her sleep. I was told it was a peaceful death, with her family at her bedside.

It was the same night that I had a vivid dream that Bernadette was in her spirit-body, flying horizontally down the long hospital corridor with a friendly smile. She passed me and then turned her head around and blew me a kiss. She said sweetly, "I love you, Carolyn. Goodbye." She looked saintly and bright as she floated away.

THE DISAPPEARING BLONDE

While her dad lay dying in his bedroom, my best friend, Sandra, didn't want to be alone with him. She called me to come over right away. Despite the raw veggie juices she blended for him daily, nothing could save him from the effects of Agent Orange that had poisoned him in the Vietnam War in the 1960s. The cancer was in its final stage now, taking yet another brave veteran.

I walked into the dark bedroom that morning and saw her dad laying there, a small man in his fifties, his fists in the air, fighting something only he could see. He mumbled things neither of us could understand. He appeared quite agitated. It was scary to see him like that, breathing so heavy and uneven, struggling for air.

Sandra's mom, Virginia, was at work, so Sandra was in charge of care-giving. I sat there watching him sputter, wildly waving his hands, while he argued with an invisible force. It looked to me like he was losing the battle, the last one of his life.

Was he bargaining with God for more time?

Sandra's pretty brown eyes spilled over, so she went

out to the kitchen for a ginger concoction she said he liked. I didn't think he would be able to drink it in the state he was in. I think she needed to leave the room for relief from his suffering. It's scary to be with someone who is dying and not be able to help them, much less save them. I felt powerless. All I could do was be present.

Sandra came back with a green glass of goo and sat on his bed. I sat on a chair with my back to the door, nervously listening to the heart monitor beep loudly while its light flashed on the electric screen.

The home hospice nurse came into the bedroom. She checked all the medical equipment.

"He seems to be taking in the medicine all right," she said to comfort Sandra, who looked concerned.

"He acts like he's in pain," Sandra said, obviously upset.

The young nurse checked the morphine meter again.

"He's getting the maximum dose," she said. "He's just fighting his death, afraid to let go. . ."

"I didn't hear you come to the front door," Sandra said, "Wasn't it locked?"

She always kept the doors locked.

"I knocked and the blonde lady let me in," the nurse

said, a little confused and surprised that we didn't know that. "She was standing here in the doorway of the bedroom looking at you."

"What blonde lady?" Sandra asked, looking puzzled.

We were both brunettes. We hadn't seen anyone standing in the doorway. There was no one in the house except the two of us until the nurse came in. With raised eyebrows, we all looked at each other.

"The lady who was here, she let me in and told me you were in the bedroom. She was just standing right *here*," the nurse said, bewildered. "Didn't you see her?"

Sandra and I looked at each other and shook our heads no to the nurse.

The matter of her dad dying was much more pressing to us than trying to figure out who unlocked the front door for the hospice nurse.

"Mom will be home soon." Sandra comforted her dad, wiping his perspiring forehead with a cool, damp cloth. He didn't look at her or respond, but kept his eyes on something above him near the ceiling. He was lying on his back, arguing loudly in gibberish. It was disturbing to see him in so much conflict. His hands were still in the air, frantically waving off a force we couldn't comprehend.

I couldn't help but think about the dying man's last wish to own a shiny new red convertible that now sat vacant in the driveway. He would never drive it again.

Then Sandra's mom, Virginia, was home early from work and entered the bedroom. She looked weary and sad as she sat on the side of her husband's bed, close to the father of their four grown children, the man she had spent most of her adult life with. She watched him deteriorate for months and now he lay ravaged and helpless before her. I couldn't hold back my tears.

Virginia leaned in closer, holding his hand. "I'm here now, my darling. I love you. It's OK to let go. We will be all right."

His movements slowed and he appeared less agitated as Virginia spoke to him soothingly. Then everything became still and profoundly silent.

We all sat and watched as a bright ray of sunlight flooded in through the window by his bed. A long light beam entered the man's body, and left out the window. It took Sandra's dad with it.

No one spoke for a long time. There were no words to express our awe.

* * *

The coroner was at the door with a gurney. Sandra thanked me for coming and ushered me out gently as she cried with her mom. I was glad I had been there.

* * *

On the day of the funeral, I prepared a large oven pan of hearty beef stew for Sandra. It was all I could think of doing to comfort my grieving friend and her family.

As I was dressing into my black attire, I noticed my dresser and the lid on my jewelry box had flipped up. I went over to close it when I saw a little piece of paper sticking out. It was usually tucked deep inside the cloth pocket in the back of the box. Now it stood out prominently. If it could talk, it would have said, "Take me with you." I lifted it out and saw that it was an old Kahlil Gibran poem I had saved. I read a small part of it:

On Death by Kahlil Gibran

"For what is it to die but to stand naked in the wind and to melt into the sun?
And what is it to cease breathing but to free the breath from its restless tides that it may rise and expand and seek God unencumbered?

Only when you drink from the river of silence shall you indeed sing.
And when you have reached the mountain top, then you shall begin to climb.
And when the earth shall claim your limbs, then shall you truly dance."

I put it into my black sweater pocket and left for the funeral.

* * *

After the military-style funeral, I arrived at Sandra's mom's house for the memorial gathering. I brought in the beef stew and gave it to Sandra.

Sandra said, "Thank you," then turned to her blonde sisters, Alison and Jill. "Were either of you here at the house the day Dad died?"

They both shook their heads no. Sandra and I exchanged glances. Then I remembered the paper in my pocket and handed the Death poem to Sandra's mom. Virginia took it from me. Later on she said, "That was very comforting to me. Thank you so much."

It wasn't me who thought of bringing it to her, I simply followed the nudge. I was glad I did.

Sandra and I never spoke again about what happened that day.

Was the disappearing blonde an angel sent to retrieve the soul of Sandra's dad? Did she keep herself hidden so she wouldn't scare us? There may be many angels among us who help us when we need them, and then quickly disappear.

AURAS APPEAR

I didn't set out to read people's auras. The auras came to me. The first time I saw them I was in my condo, sitting in my living room in Minnetonka, Minnesota in 1998. I talked and laughed with Susan, a flamboyant singer, and Nancy, a mellow mother of two, just enjoying and appreciating them as my dear friends.

Feeling relaxed and peaceful, I passively gazed up at Susan when her aura appeared. A royal sapphire blue radiated brightly from her head and shoulders, indicating a good, caring person. Then I looked at Nancy. Her aura was bright neon green, a strong healing color. Both shined more brilliantly than any colors here on Earth. I was fascinated, but didn't speak of it for fear I'd be thought a freak. It only lasted a moment, but I knew that my quest for spiritual knowledge and auras had begun.

* * *

My cousin Rich invited me to his company Christmas party which was a big to-do at Dave & Buster's Video Arcade with psychic tarot card readers, a palm reader, and an amazing Aura reading machine. I was in line to get a photograph of my aura. I felt nervous about it for fear it would reveal my heightened awareness of the spirit world, something I didn't want publicized.

The excited people in line ahead of me were commenting on the solid reds, oranges, and blues they saw on the screen in front of them. Somehow I knew from looking at the people in line that mine would be different. Sure enough, it was. When it was my turn, the aura machine operator laughed and whinnied like a pony when she saw my multiple bright colors changing constantly on the aura reading screen.

"Oh my, gosh, you're a multi-faceted being." She said it like it was a rare thing to see.

Aren't we all?

I blushed with embarrassment, not really surprised, but people were looking at me, staring at the changing colors on the screen: the freak.

"Take a deep breath and hold it for a moment."

I inhaled all the way in. Then I held my breath.

The aura lady instantly snapped the photo and we got a bright oval electric green picture, which was not the usual turquoise I had seen in the mirror, but what I felt at that second of the snapshot. I learned later that many performing artists can change their aura colors at will. My un-photographable aura was more like a rainbow dancing, reflecting many fluctuating far-fetched ideas, creative thoughts I was reluctant to share back then.

I took my disappointingly dull picture and merged with the party crowd.

* * *

I was sitting in an Alcohol and Other Drug Studies counseling class at San Diego City College with my coiffed gay friend Larry, who always wore his stylish Gucci sunglasses, even when it was cloudy outside, even indoors. We were like two little kids giggling in grade school, passing naughty notes to each other under our desks. We pretended we were making up personal ads as we listed qualities we did *not* want in a prospective date.

"Excessive acne," I wrote and discreetly handed my note to Larry.

"Poor hygiene," Larry wrote back.

We muffled our chuckles behind hand-covered mouths so the professor wouldn't hear us. Larry was better at this game than I was, evidenced by my laughing louder.

"Chronic unemployment," I wrote.

He read my note, looking less amused than I was.

His wit was beating mine, so I thought I would impress him with my elementary aura-reading trick.

"Larry, look at that girl across the room," I pointed. "I'm going to make her scratch her head." I focused on cute little Kara, a young student we didn't know.

"Huh?" He looked up from writing his next ad, and said "You what?"

"Just watch. . ." I focused on reading her aura which was easy, with a sterile white wall about a foot behind her. She sat still, paging through her textbook. I saw a sky-blue haze steam up from her head. I had learned it was a common color for compassionate counselors and other co-dependent personalities. As I stared intently at her aura, she lifted her hand, right on cue, and scratched her head above her left ear. It was exactly where I had focused my attention on her.

Larry let out a guffaw. "How did you do that?"

I felt exposed. I knew that ancient witches were burned at the stake for less. I had never shared this gift of mine with anyone until now—to my fun personal ad-writing buddy. Smiling, I wrote on his next illicit note, "Ability to make people scratch their heads."

"Do it again."

But now I felt like a circus act. I was concerned about karmic integrity and a possible boomerang effect. *Maybe I shouldn't be invading people's personal space like this if it makes them itch.* I'd done it for Larry. He was safe to share my secret with, because he had his own secrets.

But I wanted to prove to Larry it was no accident that Kara scratched her head. I focused on a man this time, a husky honor student named Juan. His aura was an illuminated aqua, greener than blue, signifying wisdom and harmony. As my focused gaze penetrated his forehead's electrical field, he scratched his eyebrow.

Larry's bleached-teeth grin grew wide below his designer shades.

I was pleased with my ability to entertain him.

Since then, as an educator and a singer, I've looked out at many large groups. I see the brightest auras, the most spiritual indigo-purple ones that were all exceptional in some way, and the darker, more negative auras that clung close to the body. I sent intentional love rays to them.

Through the years, I have seen many auras, but other times I have not. I guess it depends on whether I'm receptive or not. I can't force it. It comes easily and more often now when I simply *allow* it.

I see the stunning blues, bright teals, and sunny yellows. I have a long way to go in my studies of the aura, but I am always delighted when they show up. They're like old friends of mine, letting me know that the deeper spiritual dimension exists around and within us.

A few years later I learned that Larry's caring and sensitive blue light left much too soon. It saddened me to hear that his tender heart gave out from alcoholism. He died before he finished his certification process as an alcohol and other drug counselor.

When he had his memorial service in San Diego, I was staying in Minnesota and I cried.

Later I wondered if they cremated him in his Gucci's.

THE LOST RECEIPT

My mother and I went to a ritzy shopping mall called The Galleria in Edina, Minnesota, so she could return something expensive, but she was afraid she had lost her receipt. She kept digging in her purse but couldn't find it. She appeared frustrated and scared that she might be stuck with something she didn't want anymore.

I really wanted to help her, so I said a little prayer quietly to myself. "Dear God, please help me find that receipt." I expected divine guidance to prevail.

Then my consciousness shifted so I became aware of the wind blowing, and the easterly direction it was heading. I instantly knew that the receipt would be in the bushes off to the left side of the mall parking lot, but all I saw there was a white 8½-by-11-inch sheet of paper.

"Is it a small receipt?" I asked my mom.

"No," she replied. "It's a full size sheet of paper."

At this, I smiled and retrieved the page from under the shrubbery and happily gave the receipt to her.

"How did you know where to find it?"

"It wasn't me. We got help from the wind."

RIDING THE ROAR

An exhilarating adrenaline rush flashes through me as I view the United States flag flapping vigorously on a rooftop—from the northwest—the perfect angle for takeoff on the south shore of Medicine Lake. I hop in my Ford Explorer and head for my dad's old barn where I store all my windsurfing gear.

I lug the cumbersome forty-pound surfboard onto the roof of my SUV along with a bagged sail, boom, and mast, and tie them all down, then head for the lake as quickly as I can in rush-hour traffic. I already feel the cross breeze through my open car windows, breathing anticipation into my chest. I can't wait to windsurf!

When I reach Medicine Lake in Plymouth, Minnesota, I see another bold pioneer in the shape of a wet-suited woman wrestling with the waves as she struggles with her bright orange sail. The wind is roughly twenty-five miles per hour on this chilly April afternoon and there is white chop on the surface of the gray-blue lake. I love the scent of fresh water, Balsam Fir, and pines that surround this hidden treasure.

I quickly unload my gear and start fastening things together, the usual ritual that has my heart pumping as the wind whips my hair. The bathroom facilities are closed this early in the spring, so I change into my wet suit in the small enclosure surrounding a portable toilet which works fairly well as my makeshift dressing room when it's not too pungent.

I wriggle into my snug black wetsuit. It fits so tight that it takes time to pull up the arms and legs. Fortunately someone was smart enough to design a back zipper with an extra-long strap attached to it, for do-it-yourselfers like me. Now equipped to endure the harsh temperature, I amble like an arctic penguin to the shore and commence to windsurf the cold but inviting lake.

I look up and see an old fisherman's grin. He's standing in the water with waders up to his hips, casting his line.

"Do the fish bite when it's this windy?" I remember my lack of fish-luck at such times.

"I don't know. I guess I'll find out." He smiles, unconcerned.

With that, I carry my board and now-rigged sail to the shallow edge of the murky water and then hold it firmly as it floats and bobs on the water, which is up to my padded knees. *Hmmm, not too cold, but then I haven't fallen in yet.*

* * *

I had already windsurfed on Lake Calhoun in Minneapolis two days before, so I knew it could take your breath away when you fall in over your head.

My friend Colette had phoned me later that same night.

"Did you know you were on the news tonight for being the first windsurfer out on the lake after the ice melted?" She laughed.

"Really?"

"Yes."

"I don't watch TV. How did you know it was me?"

"I recognized your pink and green sail, and besides, who else would be that crazy?"

"You."

We giggled like sail sisters.

She was my windsurfing buddy, who often teased me that I was always trying to get her into trouble with her boss by coaxing her into leaving work early whenever the wind was blowing.

Today is a lot windier, more of a challenge, plus there are no windsurfing guys out this early in the season to save me if I get into trouble; just me and the one lady windsurfer, sporting the latest high-tech rig.

I jump onto my big wobbly board and haul up my heavy six-meter sail. Leaning back with all my weight, I pull hard with my outstretched arms on the braided rope to bring the heavy sail up out of the water where it is drowning. My sail is a neon tricolor with a transparent section to see where I'm headed. Most times I don't look through it but around it, since I am leaning so far back to balance the flapping sail. The water pours off the sail as it now stands upright.

I take off fast with the breeze in my sail pocket, and hear the rush of water roar beneath my board as my black diver's slippers grip the textured surface of the board. The sail jerks back and forth to get free and I nearly lose my grip. It's a little too loose, so I'm fighting the boom to hold her steady.

The sun is shaded by an occasional cotton-ball cloud. The cold reminds me it sure isn't July. It's just a matter of minutes before the feisty wind bashes the sail out of my hands. I somersault over the front of the board at breakneck speed, bouncing off the sail and plunging face first into the frigid water.

Reeling from the sudden fall, I know to swim quickly, to reach for the board before it blows away. I hoist my heavy, water-soaked body back onto the board. Shivering now, but safe, I still feel thrilled to be on the water. I am fully alive, riding the wind, feeling the returning sun on my dripping face. I love the feel of all my muscles being worked to capacity. I head back to shore because I need to lower the boom—the handle I hold onto and hook my harness into. It takes most of the strain off my arms. I lost control because it was set too high on the mast.

Back on shore to adjust things, I meet the only other daring windsurfer on the lake, Ann. She is lean and fortyish, taking a break on the shore, sipping a steaming something from her thermos.

"I need more upper body strength," she confides. She was struggling to pull the nautical lines on her sail so it was taut.

"I can help you with that." I get down on the ground beside Ann and her gigantic sail.

She hands me her girlie pink handy-haul tool—the

same brand as mine, the most modern piece of equipment I own. I pull her sail super tight with all my might and she is visibly pleased with my triumphant tug o' war.

"I learned to windsurf on a river in Washington," she said, taking a bite of her energy bar.

"I learned on a land simulator in San Diego, and then followed-up here on the lakes with my former fiancé's patient tutoring."

I once only dreamed of being a windsurfer.

Five years ago I stood on this same shore merely observing the exciting action out on the lake. Now I'm part of it. After several hundred unintended topples into the water, I had been more like a soaked gymnast than a wave rider, being dunked both forwards and backwards.

I was on my fourth season now, feeling rather accomplished at being intermediate. I stuck with it, even though I had taken the windsurfer walk of shame many times, towing my lagging gear in the shallows as I slumped along the shoreline. Men nodded knowingly at me and snickered. Failure was just a lesson to be learned, I decided, never a reason to give up.

"I don't know how you use those harness lines," Ann said, admiring my blue seat harness that looks like a canvas diaper, "I'm not that brave yet. I don't know how to water-start either."

"I accomplished both feats just last summer. Now I am going to learn to jibe."

"What's that?" she asked.

"Jibing is turning around real fast by throwing the sail sideways into the wind and then catching it. It's faster and more fun than tacking." I know I will also attempt her water-start, stepping onto the undulating board in deep water, using the strength of the wind to lift me up and out of the water as the board takes off at the exact same time. It's a wild ride with the wind.

I enjoy our camaraderie, but it's time to hit the water again, this time with my boom in place and a tightened sail.

I'm going to fly now.

There is something so natural and timeless about being on the water. I'm not polluting the lake with motorboat fuel or making loud noise like a jet ski. Windsurfers call them personal stinkpots. I am riding the wind, which is free, on my equipment, which is not. The water is my safety net, the catchall for clumsiness, and also the thing to avoid if you truly want to windsurf. The conditions are constantly changing out there, and the wind can backlash at any second.

I fall in again, and as I struggle to climb back up, I hear a gull laughing at me overhead.

"Oh, you think that's funny, do you?" I say to the bird as I try to position my rig for a ride. I muster up more determination. I hook the sail into my harness, lean back with more pressure than I ever have before. The wind grabs me snugly as I speed off, tearing up the surface of the undulating water. Now I am soaring and the water rushing under my board is roaring.

"Yee ha!" I squeal as I hang on for my life. By maneuvering the sail to the proper angle to the wind, I scream across the choppy waves at top speed. What a rush! Holding the boom with every ounce of strength I have, with the wind in full control, I lean back as far as I can as my butt skims the waves. The pure ecstasy of riding the roar is indescribable.

I windsurf until I'm exhausted, then I steer slowly up-wind to shore for an apple and a drink of water. The workout makes me hungry and the wind makes me thirsty. I eye the old fisherman out in the water, casting his line to nothing in particular, hooking only the waves. I relate to the old man's need to simply stand there in the water, like part of the lake, whether or not he ever gets a nibble. Some of us are nature people, in love with being a part of something greater than ourselves. I look with appreciation over the pristine lake, delighting in the sunlit sparkles that dance on the water. I'm part of that light and so is he, fish or no fish.

I spent so many evenings falling into this lake, humbled and struggling to overcome my fears and inadequacies to conquer a sport dominated by athletic, risk-taking men. Now I'm adept, with a magnificent obsession, as an enthusiastic wind-worshipper who has to get wet. It's fun to put on a one-handed acrobatic show near the shore for the waving observers. I overhear them ask each other, "Is that a woman out there?"

I see two ladies with short brown haircuts on land cheering me on in the name of feminism, as if I have just broken a world record. This isn't the first time I've pushed the limits into man land. I drove my Kawasaki 440 motorcycle for three years, even arrived at my college graduation ceremony on it, wearing my cap and gown. A group of adolescent males jeered at me through their car windows that day. I guess they thought I should be home nursing a baby or sautéing a stir fry.

"Dyke!" they screamed at me with venom.

I chuckled at their youthful ignorance. Now a competent windsurfer, I feel like I've been elevated to not only being admired by the boys, but by the lesbians themselves, an even greater honor.

Once a brave beginner, I now have the lake at my command, the great wind for power, and a passport to the arena of dangerous, high-speed sports. So what if my mascara smudges and my hair looks like Medusa's? The rebellious flicker that beats in my heart makes me feel impervious to mockery. Now I have earned official "wind snob" status. I'm a lady windsurfer who has earned my sea booties. My on-shore fans applaud and cheer for their heroine, a riotously addicted, wild windsurfing woman riding their roar.

HOW I BECAME A WINDSURFING INSTRUCTOR

While daydreaming on the warm beach one day after windsurfing at Medicine Lake, I envisioned what it would be like to teach windsurfing to others. It was a fleeting thought that felt really nice. Then my attention turned to other things. A few minutes later, a young man, who saw my wet sail lying next to me on the ground, walked up to me. He was about thirty with broad shoulders and saggy swim trunks.

"Is it hard to windsurf?" he asked.

"Would you like to try it? I can teach you." I smiled.

He smiled broadly and stood up straight and ready.

"Sure!" He followed me as I lugged my big beginner surfboard to the water's edge. I steadied the board for him, and he eagerly hopped on. He stood on the bobbing board in the swampy shallows, awaiting instructions. I showed him my three-step process of balancing, pulling back, and then leaning away from the sail. He listened intently. I now had my first student, immediately after imagining it.

He tugged at the boom. The sail lurched. He took off. "Woo hoo!" he squealed.

I watched in amazement as his knees bent, his feet gripped the tippy board, and he actually hung on. Most everyone who tries it the first time falls. He didn't.

That day I became a proud windsurfing instructor for brave beginners. I wonder if mama ducks feel the same pride when their fluffy ducklings make it over tumultuous waves without sinking.

I taught him and two more people after that, getting my teaching system down pat. My technique worked very well so I started charging for my surf-starter services, while supplying the windsurfing equipment. It all began with a daydream. What a fun summer job it turned out to be. *If only summer could last.*

Then I dreamed of moving away from Minnesota and living in sunny San Diego, California where my cousin, Rich, lived. Winter always came too soon and lasted too long. My Grandma Grace's ghost came to me in a night dream and whispered, "You're a summer bird."

Then I wrote a poem and an essay about my winter blues to express my feelings to my close relatives, who I would soon be leaving.

MY WINTER WINDOW

Holiday winds of bitter freeze

Where chattering teeth

Meet clattering knees

At my door with a tattered Christmas wreath

I'm moving to California

Midwest Folks: "Don't you fear?"

They don't know how much

I dislike it here.

The traffic dance is Siberian crawl

Icy hills—a haul to the top

Driving down bumpy iced roads

Praying, "God help me stop!"

The trees wave and whistle

Their agony tunes

The landscape becomes

A desert of ruins

Shivering dog in deep snow wades

Howls like a plea for a warmer day

The morning whirr of snow-blower blades

Clears twenty-six inches of snow away

Sad black trees against a gray sky canvas

Crystalline-white blankets of sparkles below

A masterpiece of stark contrast

The only art from my winter window.

WINTER A-VERSION

A January appraisal of my native Minnesota

I am not a jolly admirer of crystalline snow-scapes. I am more inclined to throw a snowball at Old Man Winter than pretend to remain in seven months of frigid contentment. Arriving back home at the Minneapolis-Saint Paul airport from a warm tropical retreat, something in my gut snapped, and it wasn't my too-tight ski pants.

I wanted out.

As a native Minnesotan, I should be used to the annual winter goose bumps, chicken skins, or whatever frozen bird you prefer, to describe raised pores that try to shake off the shiver. I was still fighting off the chill from the killing wind after being inside my heated house for twenty minutes.

I slipped on the icy driveway the second I stepped out of my car and injured my tailbone. Welcome home to Eden Prairie. Now I'm focused on indoor dust balls cowering in the corners, picking fuzzies off my red sweater, and eating a hearty hot dish that makes me feel as bulky as a winter coat.

I don't enjoy breathing artificial heat from a dry furnace or being shocked when my unsuspecting fingers touch metal. With static fly-away hair, I compare my Mexican "Yucca" tan to my white sister Northerners at the YMCA. I see how unflattering their neon-white, glow-in-the-dark skin is, especially flakey legs that beg for a swim season shave.

Even worse are the overcooked tanners. They flaunt fake sunburn like they just flew in from Acapulco. They are probably nursing sore, burnt butts from the newly installed brighter bulbs at the tanning booth. This is winter entertainment consequences for closeted Caucasians who pay to get nuked naked.

I'm home, ready to eat my steaming casserole (a hot dish combo of meat, vegetables, and cream-of-anything soup). I carry it to the living room couch to catch a ho-hum TV show. A lean cat body weaves through my ankles, throwing me off balance, toppling me into the pink Christmas cactus. Fortunately, they don't have thorns. But my saucy dinner is now carpet topping. My hyper stir-crazy cats dart around the house like hockey pucks, clawing out the wall insulation through holes they made trying to get out. I won't let them out or they will morph into darling ice statues.

Winter means yanking at my strangling turtleneck tops, walking in unbendable knees inside frumpy long johns, and being wrapped in a heavy down parka just to walk to my mailbox.

Chapped himself, my lover surely enjoys kissing my dry, cracking lips that bleed a little bit when I smile, which I don't do a whole lot in January. It's one of the worst weather months of the year in Minnesota.

At the mall I see outdated shoulder-padded sweaters turn petite women into linebackers. Shopping and overeating are favorite winter pastimes. Extra fat is needed to pad Minnesota thighs—thus the bigger bumper on our bedeviled behinds, a necessary buffer from the blizzards. Sweatshirts are the fashion mode for most Minnesotans on weekends, with every kind of hokey message emblazoned on front. Vanity is quickly abandoned in favor of warmth.

The food conditions are worse. The shipped-in tomatoes are hard and pink. Oranges look green, and my favorite summer ice cream is "*out of season?*" Mugs of hot chocolate are more of a hand warmer than a high-calorie beverage.

My deprived indoor mind overdoses on escapist

television and self-help books, after-holiday sale shopping, and impeccable housekeeping since we are all stuck in the house. My mom searches for my kids' uncoupled mittens, then sweeps the tracked-in street salt in the doorway. Dad trips over the buried snow shovel in the driveway after filling up his four by four's radiator tank with anti-freeze. The kids fight over their turn playing video games, rubbing runny noses on their flannels, and innocently beg me to go sledding outside in thirteen-below wind-chill. Uh, the answer is no.

The loud furnace-blown heat is literally saving our lives as it spreads flu germs around my family. Unwelcomed winter is here, and it's time to hibernate until springtime cheerfully whisks the doors open. Or a miracle occurs and I can somehow move to California.

BAND INTENTIONS

I needed a night out, so I drove to a little rib joint in Bloomington, Minnesota, because I heard they had dancing there with no cover charge. On the way, I was daydreaming about how I wanted to do more with my music. I knew I could sing, but how would I ever get started? All I had done was a little karaoke. I knew I was capable of so much more.

I parked, which wasn't easy, and slid into the crowd to find a table just as a group was leaving. I sat there for only a moment when someone grabbed my arm, rather forcefully, and asked, "Do you want to dance?"

Before I had a chance to answer him, he lifted me up by my arm and led me to the dance floor. If I had said no he might have still taken my arm with him. So we danced together.

"My name is Samir," he said smiling with a scary gold tooth glistening. He sounded Mid-eastern.

"I'm Carolyn."

He was in my space bubble, so close I could smell garlic on his breath. He wasn't my type, too aggressive, but I didn't want to sit in that booth alone all night either. We danced quickly then came back to the table, both of us a little sweaty.

"What do you do for fun?" he asked, sliding his chair closer to my side. His aftershave needed updating. I moved my head to one side and coughed, then faced him.

"I sing karaoke," I said, leaning away from his bristling bold chin, "I have a business as a karaoke host."

He unexpectedly grabbed my arm again, and practically dragged me across the room to the front of the stage, directly to the bandleader, a balding middle-aged rocker, who was setting up his music equipment on stage. I was stunned by my escort's boldness and spontaneity.

"She can *sing*." He pointed at me, presenting me to the band's lead singer.

"What songs do you know?" he asked as he bent over, plugging in an electrical cord.

"Can I see your set list?" I said nervously, trying to muster some courage. I was told to "act as if, until you gain confidence." I was acting as if I were a real singer.

"Sure." He handed me a nicely printed list of his band's songs. I didn't know anything. Then, near the end, was a song I was sort of familiar with—the melody at least.

"I know *Stand by Me.*" I blurted out before he changed his mind. I didn't really know the song, but when an opportunity shows up, I take it and figure out how to do it later.

"OK, come up right after the break, and you can sing that one," he said, turning his back to continue setting up. Samir, my aggrandizing Middle Eastern angel left me there, maybe to go find another female arm to capture.

Here was my opportunity. Now what?

The band didn't see how surprised and excited I looked. I turned back to my table that had been overtaken by rowdy frat boys. My giddy celebratory feeling quickly morphed into stage fright.

Oh my God, I don't really don't know that song.

I sat down alone at the bar, armpits dripping, heart beating fast. I grabbed a little cocktail napkin off the bar where I scribbled lyrics to "Stand by Me" as fast as I could. I sang it softly to myself over and over, even checked in with others around me, asking people how it went. This was way before we had smart phones to turn to.

I looked around. The place was packed. *Oh my God, I'm going to sing tonight. Please God, help me remember the words and the timing. Thank you, God.*

"Ladies and gentlemen, we have a guest singer here tonight, Miss Carolyn James…"

My last name was always getting mispronounced, but I didn't care. I was going to sing! It was the beginning of the second set and I hopped up onto the big stage quickly, acting as if I did this all the time, clutching my damp napkin in my shaky left hand for security.

I took the microphone and sang *Stand by Me* with my whole soul to a full house. They applauded wildly. After that, I was a real singer. I had intended to do more with my music, but I didn't think it would happen so fast. It did. Our thoughts are powerful. And passing earth angels who lead us to our opportunities come in all races, ages, and nationalities.

SETTING SAIL FOR SAN DIEGO

I was all set to leave Minnesota, where I had lived for forty-one years, to head for my California dream relocation. I had sold my house, and donated or packed all my belongings and furniture except for six really old nylon windsurfing sails that hung in my otherwise empty garage.

How in the world would I get rid of them?

I can't toss them into any trash dumpsters. They won't fit. The male-elite windsurfers I knew all wanted the latest and greatest high-tech sails. My sails were far too ancient to sell or even give away.

Sitting by peaceful Lake Calhoun that July afternoon, I pondered how I could get rid of these hopelessly outdated sails. The weight of the problem baffled me. Then I let go of it and relaxed on my Mexican beach blanket.

A kindly old gentleman plopped down beside me on the grass. He talked excitedly about the windsurfers as we watched them cruise over the chop on the lake. He appeared to be a big fan of the sport.

Then he casually mentioned, "I make things out of

old sails."

I couldn't believe it. *What were the odds of this happening?*

"I have six free sails for you at home in my garage!"

He followed me home, gladly took the granddaddy sails off my hands, and I was amazingly unencumbered and ready to leave town for San Diego, California.

* * *

I drove solo all the way to the Pacific Ocean. My concerned grandmother's voice echoed in my head, "What will you *do* out there?"

"Whatever God wants me to . . ."

ROUTE 66

After working hard to learn all the new song lyrics for a San Diego rhythm and blues band I had just joined, I was feeling discouraged as a new singer. I had just moved to the West Coast alone, and I missed my family and longtime friends who still lived in Minnesota. I was afraid my singing career was a naïve, silly dream and I desperately needed some direction.

I was taking a leisurely walk along the Pacific Beach boardwalk when I thought, *Am I on the right path? Am I supposed to be in California pursuing a singing career? Please God, give me a sign and let me know if I'm doing the right thing.*

I asked God this question and then became aware of a jogger running past me. He wore a white T-shirt that had a *Route 66* logo imprinted on the back. I began to cry in recognition of this personal symbol. It was one of the band songs I was just rehearsing in my headphones. The lyrics also mark the highway's city points all the way from the Midwest to California.

It was the route I had driven to get to San Diego!

I received the perfect answer, with that sign addressing both of my burning questions in one fleeting glimpse. I went back to my diligent practice, now content I was on the right track.

COUPE DE VILLE BAND

Smiley on the piano
T-Bone on guitar
Sax-man blowin' blues
The Singer, I'm the Star
Bass Guy booked the band
The audience drinks their wine
Found I loved their music
When I heard them the first time
Stunning how well they jammed
Spicy hot music with fire
Casinos and upscale hotels
The kind of venues that hire
Blues and rhythmic funky beats
Attracting people off the streets
Something tasty for the soul
Catchy classic rock and roll
This is my West Coast band
I'll perform and light up the stage
And promote this little endeavor
'Til my band becomes the rage.

MY PERFECT COTTAGE

After finding a lot of vodka bottles in her condo cupboards, my live-in landlady seemed a little nutty. The first day that we became house mates, I woke up to her standing over me in her underwear, talking to me as if nothing was weird about that. In that small one-bedroom condo I had no privacy even though my bed was in the upstairs living area that she said she never went into. I was intent on moving out soon, but wasn't sure what to look for. I wanted my savings to hold out as long as possible.

I looked at recreational vehicles, apartments, and other roommate situations. Nothing worked out. California rents were high. The places I could afford were dumpy, already taken, or too small to spin around in.

I was having trouble, so I asked God in a prayer, "Please help me find my own place."

That afternoon I called on a one bedroom cottage the day after the ad came out in the paper. Often I didn't get return phone calls on the messages I left, but this time a man called me back quickly. I was able to see it that Friday afternoon.

Roomy and sunlit, with freshly painted walls and bleached porcelain sinks, the little cottage was just what I was looking for, with a little garden space in the back. The rent was less than the comparable apartments I had seen.

I put down a deposit that same day and moved in the following Monday, just three days later–*without a job or any verifiable income.*

The owner accepted me on my good credit and my creative ideas to improve the garden.

There was a lemon and a persimmon tree in the back yard for picking. Additionally, I had grumbled too many times about the poor water pressure in the previous condo. This new bath had a massive shower head, great water pressure, and a heat lamp built in to the ceiling. *God knows me.* There was enough space for everything, hardwood floors, new appliances, and a yellow-tiled kitchen I adored.

Soon I would even have a roommate.

RAYMOND THE PSYCHIC

My caregiver cap was on the day we met, and Raymond, being psychic, must have known it. His name was appropriate, since he was black, slick, and mysterious. Facing eviction from his deceased mother's estate, he glommed onto me for a quick place to live. All I saw were his gorgeous brown eyes all a-glimmer, not the glom. Handsomeness trumped his homelessness.

Have you ever met anyone whose presence was so loud you couldn't hear what they were saying? Raymond's undecipherable words entered my infatuated ears like a sexy foreign language, even though his English was more proper than mine. I kept turning my ears this way and that, like antennae, trying to interpret the utterances from his thick, luscious lips, but it was a garbled conglomerate of tantalizing sensuality and total gobbledygook.

We roller-skated gracefully as a couple at Mission Bay, our bodies in synch, our sexual synergy stirred up. That was all the communication I required.

Later I learned he had a multiple-personality disorder, a mental illness (now termed *dissociative disorder)* but at this early introduction I considered him a possible roommate.

I needed help with my rent so after only three days, I moved him into my one-bedroom cottage. Yes, he could share my bed too. I was either that broke at the time, or he was just that irresistible—the epitome of a taboo lover: an unemployed stranger, a different race, a hidden past, and my family would hate him.

One morning he handed me four hundred dollars for half of our rent, and then he warned me about an impending accident that day.

"Be aware," he said with pleading eyes. "There will be a black SUV on the road today. The driver is distracted. She's going through a divorce and she won't see you. Please be careful."

"Really? How weird. OK, I'll keep an eye out."

As a professional singer, I was used to traveling on the San Diego highways going from gig to gig, and as I ran my errands that day I was aware of all the colors of the cars around me. So many California cars were *white*. Then I forgot all about his prediction until later that afternoon.

I was cruising south on Highway 15 after my singing engagement, when suddenly a monstrous dark blob came at me from the right side of my peripheral vision, careening into my lane at a high speed, an inch away from my seemingly now thin passenger door.

I quickly veered to the left to avoid a collision.

Suddenly Raymond's warning came back to me. He was right. It was definitely an SUV–black, too. I didn't see the driver at all. I didn't need to. I was shaken, but safe. Raymond knew it would happen, and I knew he was gifted.

Little did I know there was a whole lot more to him.

THE INVISIBLE LIFE SAVER

Raymond was driving my SUV down the interstate highway at the speed limit, along steep mountain curves with only rocks all around us, when our right front wheel fell off our car. It flew high up into the air, then bounced somewhere into a deep canyon on the right side of the narrow mountain road. Our Ford Explorer was headed for the dangerous sharp left curve ahead.

Sparks flew as the three-wheeled car careened out of control. Raymond and I looked at each other, thinking we were doomed to die. *It looks like this is it.* We were prepared to be killed together right then. But someone had other plans. Time either stopped or we went into slow motion. Somehow our vehicle was miraculously lifted up and then gently set down exactly in the one-car length parking space on the otherwise shoulder-less mountain road. We came to a peaceful, silent halt. The dust settled. We sat there astonished, looking at each other in shock.

How did we go from sure death to a safe stop?

We gathered ourselves and prayed together. "Thank you God for saving us. Now can you please find our tire?"

The canyon must have been fifty feet deep with nothing but huge immovable rocks as far as the eye could see. It was an amazing view, but a very difficult hike.

How on earth would we get our lost wheel back in this rocky mountain canyon?

I told Raymond I would pray for direction. "Dear God, please help him find our tire." Even if he *did* find it, which seemed impossible in that bumpy terrain, how could he even carry that heavy wheel up through all that jumbled geology?

I prayed as Raymond climbed down the steep slope, walked about thirty yards and went *directly* to the runaway wheel and retrieved it from behind a giant boulder. Raymond hoisted it up on his wide shoulders and carried it back. I was dumbfounded. The wheel was not at all visible from where we were standing on the highway. Yet he walked right to it.

Our prayers had been answered.

Raymond was an auto mechanic, so he quickly removed one lug nut from each of the remaining three wheels, and used them to secure the newfound fourth wheel onto the front of our car. We then continued our long drive to Phoenix, grateful for the help we received.

Later that evening, I phoned my helpful cousin Rich, who had given me a free brake job that morning in his driveway. I told him what happened.

"We were almost killed, but God or an angel saved us."

He admitted that when he replaced my brake pads he had forgotten to re-tighten the lug nuts one last time before I drove off.

"If God helped you, why didn't He just tighten the lug nuts?" Rich teased.

"Ah, that was *your* job."

A MAN, MULTIPLIED

Right before we broke up, Raymond was at the casino every night, chasing his next big win on the slot machines. As psychic as he was about cars and me, he was delusional when it came to video poker. Raymond tried to earn money gambling professionally because he couldn't hold a job with his multiple personalities that kept changing his direction. I couldn't count them all, but I'm sure they were there. Most of the time he was like a nurturing mammy, spoiling me like I was his child, lovingly washing my hair, cooking the best barbecued ribs ever, and folding my laundry into perfect piles.

One of his personalities was a savvy, smooth-talking businessman trying to manage me as a singer and cut me a big recording deal in Los Angeles. He even had an official-looking cookie-cutter (fake) legal contract he printed off the Internet—for authenticity. After he produced my original compact disk with his best songwriter friend, he tried to convince me he would then produce my next big concert. It was exciting to think about and I believed he could make it happen. He seemed so capable, but his compulsive lying must have finally choked him because I saw him puke in a parking lot in Hollywood after trying to convince an influential man at Capital Records to sign me as an artist.

The scariest personality I saw in him was the black leather jacket-wearing one, The Thug, a street-smart thief, and a gambling addict I didn't like, who bragged that he had beat someone up in his past.

Of course he couldn't get a job. His confident business side would set up the job interview on the phone, The Mammy would press his shirt, and then the scared, incompetent one would leave for the appointment with his head down. I despaired, knowing he couldn't get any job as that man.

His early childhood abuse from a babysitter had scarred him. He appeared to lack insight for the need to integrate these many sides of his complex personality. I don't think he was consciously trying to con anyone, since he didn't know he had all these compartments. He just thought he had a lousy memory. I loved him, but I couldn't help him. I felt stressed out by him every single day. Even though he was always very kind and loving to me, things were getting worse.

When Raymond wasn't at the casino playing his slot machines, he was home playing loud war-shooting video games all night to distract himself. I knew something wasn't right when he stole my ten speed bike from our house, blaming it on an intruder who climbed in through the tiny bathroom window.

After that, I hid my cash and credit cards from him. He wasn't home much after that. I worried about him, and I worried about me.

One night Raymond called me. I heard muffled casino bells clanging in the background. He said he was at a friend's house and would be home late. When he finally arrived home in the morning, he said he had run out of gas. *Twice.* Fed up with his ridiculous stories, I locked him out of the house, and put his things on the doorstep. I knew he wasn't going to stop gambling, not even for me. He had already refused to go back to Gamblers Anonymous after his first meeting. Raymond had told the recovering gamblers there that they sure had problems and he was glad he wasn't like *them.*

A recovered old-timer there took me aside. "Honey, if you don't leave him, he will take you down the toilet too."

I was done. So I moved out of state to cut the cord.

* * *

I credit Raymond with teaching me more than I ever wanted to know about compulsive gambling. How could I have been played so casually like one of his video poker games? He was bluffing himself. How could he stand to hang out in that smoke-filled casino with the stench of body odor from the underarms of little old ladies with nickel bags, and grungy gray men, jerking on levers all night?

And how much money had he lost over the years? Were the sounds of those blaring bells blurring out his dire past?

When our romantic roller-skating relationship ended after eight months, I had nice souvenirs; his good recipes, a nice turquoise planter from his mother's foreclosed property, and a compact disk, The Sky's The Limit, that he produced just for me.

It's a miracle that he managed to record our original music.

POETIC LESSON

I loved a cutie named Raymond

So sexy I wanted to stay in

We rented a one-bedroom rambler

'Til he revealed to me he was a gambler

I got out then so I wouldn't cave in.

The Gambler

I met a gambler with a losing hand

Who clung to me like a dying man

He played upon my true compassion

I took him in (in sympathetic fashion)

He lost all the money he had for our rent

Then made up stories on how it was spent

He lied every time he moved his lips

Denying the slots at his fingertips

I crave escape from this survival rut

I tiptoe on egg shells, knots in my gut

How could I be so naïve not to see?

All this time he was deceiving me

Placing bets he thought were a shoe-in

'Til I asked him to leave to avoid complete ruin

The Casino strategy: Treat him like a Star

How regal are you when you sleep in your car?

Gamblers Anonymous, we went to a meeting

They welcomed us with a warm greeting

I talked about this man I love very much

Who's in so much pain, and out of touch

Now all I can do is stay busy and wait

He'll either quit gambling, or we'll separate

Is he going to stop now, placing his bets?

Or leave me alone to pay all our debts

I know he's feeling incredible shame

He hides out, avoids it, and shifts all the blame

Penniless, broken, all he owns is his name

What now is rock bottom was once just a game.

BABY, PLEASE

Baby, please stop what you're doin'
You know it only leads to ruin
You're on a path of self-destruction
You've gotten so low that you can't function

I'm the woman who can handle you
Now you're afraid I'll saddle you
I already love you. You don't have to lie
I want you so please give truth a try

Your love has launched a sneak attack
I'm with you now, there's no going back
You have my whole heart; while you give a fraction
Now you are lost, as you drown in distraction

Baby, please give up what's eating you
You simply can't win–it's beating you
It's a progressive deadly affliction
You can't love both me and your addiction.

ORVIE'S ANTICS

Orvie was my pipe-smoking, black licorice-loving, wise-cracking Grandpa. I remember him singin', "I like to go swimmin' with bowlegged women…" My daughter, Natalie, said all she remembers is that I covered her ears whenever he came into the room. He lived in Spooner, Wisconsin—far from his Minnesota family.

Ever since Orvie's Wife, Sally died, he kept a framed picture in his living room of her grinning cutely with her legs straddling a concrete donkey cart, pretending to ride in it. My aunt Diane loved this funny photo because she had a similar donkey cart, a wooden flower planter on her front lawn that she bought on one of her visits to see Orvie.

My aunt Diane, my mom, and my brother Tim were planning to make the two and a half hour drive to Spooner on Sunday to take Orvie out to dinner for Father's Day. On the Wednesday before, Aunt Diane called him to confirm their plans.

"I will see you Sunday, Dad," she said.

"I'm not feeling well," he admitted.

"Would you like me to come out sooner and help you?"

"Oh no," he reassured her. "I'll see you on Father's Day."

"I wish you could come and see my garden," she said as the call ended.

Grandpa Orvie died that night.

Diane got the sad news and cried alone in her house. She couldn't sleep. She woke up at 3:33 a.m. on Father's Day to loud music playing somewhere in her house. Scared, she groggily walked downstairs to the small spare room where her radio was blaring old time music, the kind Orvie had loved to dance to. It wasn't her radio station. She recalled seeing him dance just three weeks earlier. She thought it was odd, but she was so tired, she turned off the radio and went back to bed.

In the morning, Diane walked to her living room window and pulled open the drapes like she did every day. She looked out at her front lawn. Something was missing. Where her donkey cart planter used to be, there was now an empty space in her yard. Diane panicked because it's where she hid her house key. She thought someone might have been in her house overnight. She looked around and saw that the donkey cart had mysteriously moved to the middle of her asphalt driveway. It hadn't been there when she came home late the night before, or she would have run over it. Diane ran outside to check on the house key and it was still there, undisturbed. But how on earth did her heavy donkey cart get on her driveway?

Later that day, Diane went outside to her garden. She thought about how much she had wanted Orvie to see her well-tended flowers. Then she realized that maybe the oldies music and the donkey cart were signs that Orvie had been there. This gave her great relief, comfort, and strength that Orvie was all right. He had let her know that he had indeed seen her garden on Father's Day.

* * *

My mom told me that she had been reading about the famous psychoanalyst, Carl Jung. He had coined the term "synchronicity" which means meaningful coincidences. He once treated a very depressed patient who wasn't getting well. Dr. Jung and his female patient randomly discussed an Egyptian scarab beetle in her therapy session. Just then a big black beetle appeared outside the office window. This amazing coincidence so convinced the patient of synchronicity, that she made great progress in her therapy after that.

My mom, a psychology major, was so struck by the strange beetle story, that she us all about it.

On the night Grandpa Orvie died, my mom and her husband, Jim, awoke at the same time to an odd scratching sound in their bedroom. Turning on the light, they looked to see where the sound was coming from. They were shocked to see a big black bug on their dresser—a beetle! They had never seen one in the house before. Suddenly the scarab beetle story came to mind. Jim picked up the beetle and put it in a jar. They later read that it was sometimes called "a death watch beetle." The following night, mom found out Orvie had died. When she heard the news, her sister Diane said that she had a dream about Orvie. In her dream, he said, "Tell Janet, 'Good-bye.'"

* * *

On Father's Day, in the middle of the night, I awoke reluctantly to insistent tapping on the wooden headboard of my bed. It was a loud rhythmic pounding like a type of Morse code. Apparently, Orvie's spirit was making his rounds. I felt his masculine energy in the room and sensed the aroma of his sweet cherry tobacco.

I asked out loud, "Grandpa, is that you?"

The tapping got faster, like he was excited that I knew he was there, and then the tapping stopped.

I asked him, "Do you want me to sing *Wind Beneath My Wings* at your funeral?"

The tapping started again, loud and frantic.

With that, I said, "OK then, I will."

Then his energy left my room.

* * *

I set up my music speakers and sound amplifier at Orvie's funeral chapel. I was afraid I might lose my composure during the song, even though I had sung *Wind Beneath My Wings* hundreds of times professionally. This was different though. This was my own family. I felt more emotionally exposed than I ever have with any audience.

Orvie had helped me buy my house in Minnesota which I later sold, enabling me to move to San Diego and live my dreams as a singer. The same lyrics suddenly took on deeper meaning as my grieving lungs exhaled the words: "Did you ever know that you're my hero? And everything I would like to be. I can fly higher than an eagle, for you are the wind beneath my wings."

I got through the song without crying, but as soon as it was over, I wailed for my grandpa who was the wind beneath my West Coast dreams. After my performance, seeing my tears, my male relatives kindly helped me carry my heavy speakers and pack my car.

Weak from grief, I sat outside the chapel on a wooden bench and admired the dainty white flowers waving at me. I recalled all the signs we had seen—my mom's big black beetle, Aunt Diane's mysterious moving donkey cart, her changed radio dial with big band music, and my tapping experience of Orvie's antics in my room. He wanted me to sing *this* song for our family. With tears in my eyes, I looked up at the puffy clouds and saw a bright light shining through them. With gratitude for all he had done for me I said, "Thank you, Grandpa." I smiled then, imagining Orvie reunited with his wife Sally, dancing in heaven.

CELESTIAL MUSIC

Have you heard the Celestial music?
It is filled with so much love
Like a thousand angels singing
In our hearts, in heaven above
I could explode from the impact
Of receiving so much grace
God opens our hearts even wider
To hold more love in place
I was asleep in a joyous dream
When the Divine music came to me
I awoke in amazing, blissful awe
That such loveliness could even be
Heavenly Hosts surround us
Protecting us with care
Summon Spirit's sacredness
For it is always there
Passionately seek thy innocence
With childlike wonder and glee
Your heart will dance and sing with joy
To know it's One with Thee.

SMELLING LIKE A ROSE

In just one day, I lost my job, my home, and my fiancé. After one of the top ten worst days of my life, my friend Cheri said in retrospect, "No matter what happens to you, Carolyn, you come out smelling like a rose."

She only saw the rainbow results, not the stormy predicaments I waded through. What looked to her like a smooth swim was to me a whirlwind of chaotic, unplanned, zigzag changes. She saw a tidy straight line to an upgraded life. I felt propelled by a hurricane.

I didn't panic when I lost these things and my lover. I checked myself into a Super 8 Motel—my solitary psych ward—to grieve, chill out, and get some quiet time with God. I wrote out my mixed feelings in my journal, (confusion, anger, sadness, relief) and called my friends to vent. I slept and tried to regroup from the sudden, painful, and overwhelming shock.

Slowly I recognized that my prayers had actually been answered.

I had asked God to be relieved of my live-in House Manager position at a women's sober living home owned by a loud lady, in favor of my own quiet space and privacy, and I asked for clarity around my dating relationship with my former fiancé, Kirk, that had dead-ended. I got these answers all at once and my life changed swiftly. Manifestations can be super-sonic sometimes.

The next day I heard a commanding voice inside my head say, "Get up and check for housing on Craigslist."

But it's only six am!

Protesting, I wearily rolled over on my soggy, mascara-smudged pillow. I felt exhausted from grief, but the inner voice was insistent. I relented. I knew I needed a place to live—fast.

I went online, checked Craigslist, and found a picture of a darling one-bedroom house I could afford to rent on a small horse ranch. I showered, got dressed, and dragged myself, blurry-eyed, to the outskirts of Lakeside that morning. I was interviewed by the congenial property manager, and somehow qualified for it on my credit alone, without a job.

This is when I *know* my Higher Power is running the show, because it goes so positively perfect, so stunningly smooth, and contrary to my own circular thinking. It flows effortlessly. I did nothing to make it happen, except listen.

Be receptive, follow my hunch, and act on it. That's how it works for me.

After five nights in my hotel room, I moved into my own quaint farmhouse, with its big windows and earthy aroma from the corral, near my tranquil new neighbors, a horse and a pony.

Next, in a prayer, I asked God, "What should I do for work?"

Nothing else I tried had worked out for very long. I would end up leaving a job after just a few months, knowing it wasn't right for me. I asked what would be recession-proof, needed in the market, was in a growing field, something I could do well with joy, and be fully self-supporting.

I got a very clear message that night in bed, "Caregiver."

I called an acquaintance, Jane, who was a *Jane of all trades*, like me.

"What are you doing for work now?"

"I'm a private caregiver," Jane said.

Aha!

"There is a caregiver training this Saturday, do you want to come?" she asked me.

Since I was open to anything, I said yes, even though I had no background in nursing or care-giving, but within a short time I increased my income from my last job, and God put me where my latent talents were needed. When I asked to be placed in my next assignment, I had no preconceived picture, no expectations, or plan of what it should look like. I was just completely open, simply willing to do God's will. Surrendering control of my life is about giving up *my will* to God, taking a back seat to guidance and then following the inner voice that nudges me to turn *right*, even when my logical mind insists I best go left. I go right, despite the objections of others around me, and then we are all surprised when somehow, miraculously, it all works out in the best possible way—a way I never would have conjured up myself.

My mantra is "God's will be done, *not* mine." This is surrender in action, and it is not for the fearful, the weak-hearted, or the faithless (the old me) as it requires a strong kind of rock-hard belief in a loving higher power that says "Close your eyes and jump!" This solid faith is built upon all the smaller miracles that occurred before the bigger, showier ones. What I believe, I see. It's not the other way around. I believe God can and will help me with anything, even if my limited mind can't figure it out. I can't count all the times this faith has worked for me.

"Yes, I'd love to go to the caregiver training," I told Jane. I smiled to myself as I sensed the universe was again having its way with me.

My former fiancé, Kirk, had been alarmed when I suddenly quit my toxic job, so afraid in fact that he back-peddled on our wedding date. It was then I realized he didn't believe in me, that he was scared, and he didn't trust me or understand my ability to manifest my intentions to secure a better job. I wanted out of that low vibe. In fact, I felt I had to leave to be true to myself.

Relationships are about trust, learning, and growth. No one knows my path better than I do, except God. When I align myself with my Higher Power's will, it all works out. No human being can be my Higher Power. They can't see my purpose or my path, or know what God's will is for me. How can they? They are human too.

I can't let others set conditions, standards, or judge me for being who I am. I learned not to believe what other people think or say about me, because they can only judge me through their own narrow mental filter. I am not here to live up, *or down*, to anyone else's expectations. I have to follow my own heart.

Whatever happens, according to my friend Cheri, I still seem to come out smelling like a rose. Sure I do, long after I wash off all that caked-on mud from the compost pile and the jolting trot through an unplowed plot, to finally bloom victorious.

TAKING CARE OF PETER

I wonder what it would be like to live in one of those luxury condos up on those cliffs. I pondered this on a glorious summer morning in California as I lazily meandered along secluded Solana Beach, which means "sunny beach" and wow, it sure was. I looked up and briefly contemplated living up on the edge of that high cliff, overlooking the wavy blue sea. It was just a fleeting thought, but it felt wonderful to daydream. *I bet living there would be fantastic.* I never dreamed it would actually materialize. I smiled and continued on my way along the rocky shoreline, feeling very *Solana* with the soft warm sand cushioning my bare feet.

* * *

Later that summer, I attended a professional caregiver training over two weekends, and a week after that, I had my first client, a kindly British gentleman named Peter, a *dream* client.

I was grieving the break-up with my fiancé, Kirk, at the time, so I wasn't in the best mental shape to think about, much less negotiate, the compensation or employment terms. However, the savvy agent that hired me secured a good rate for me without any of my input. I was satisfied with that, and grateful to have rewarding work to focus on.

I met the elderly Brit, who was to be my patient, while he convalesced in the hospital. Peter had fallen down the staircase in his home while drinking and suffered a traumatic brain injury. When I met him he was in a hospital bed and could hardly talk. Soon he whipped himself around the ward in a wheelchair, smiling boyishly up at the pretty nurses who cared for him. As serious as his condition was, he didn't appear to take it seriously at all.

His wife, Hara, on the contrary, always appeared distraught. She hadn't fully recovered from finding him at the bottom of the stairs in a pool of blood, holding his head to keep his blood from spewing out. She appeared more traumatized than he was. Her nervous green eyes often filled with tears, her Irish-looking face framed with big brownish freckles and short red hair.

Peter needed twenty-four hour care and supervision, and his wife was not exactly in holy matrimony around doing the care-giving herself. Wealth allows one to hand off one's marriage vow of "for better or worse" to a third party when it's at its worst. In fact, from what I witnessed later, it appeared that she may have been close to divorcing this former fighter pilot and leaving the celebrated war hero for good, when he fell to his near-death.

I guess she could not, in good conscience, leave him after that.

Peter and I would stay together in what Hara called "a little rental place near his rehab facility," where he would attend physical therapy Monday through Friday from nine to three, so he could learn to walk again. I was to stay with him all evening, prepare his meals, do his housekeeping, dispense his medications, and keep him safe. Hara feared another bad fall so I was to accompany him everywhere he went, to catch him when he teetered like a toddler.

Imagine my amazement when the place we were given the keys to was the same luxury condo complex I had looked up at so longingly just a few months earlier.

As Peter's private caregiver, I filled in around the clock providing supervision and non-medical services. I slept in a separate guest bedroom with a baby monitor near my ear. I was at his *beck*, and he didn't even have to call. If I heard a mere groan I hurried in with his pain pill.

The cliff-side condo was tastefully decorated, clean, and comfortably homey with a full ocean view. The fresh salty air infiltrated the sunlit western window screens. Coast guard helicopters flew outside the dining room window at eye level. A magnificent view of wispy pastel sunsets entertained us at dinner time. It was like heaven to me.

The groceries Peter asked me to purchase and prepare were all overpriced packaged gourmet foods and easy to fix. I ate with him at the table after heating our meals. He was easy going, humorous, and wise. A lover of ginger candy, he appeared seventyish with a full head of white hair and had a relaxed approach to everything. He smiled a lot despite his poor memory, unsteady gait, and speech difficulties. He was slowly improving. *So was I.*

Over time, we developed a special bond while I cared for him during his rehab, like a dutiful daughter, protecting him from falling by walking arm in arm along the beach, sharing jokes, and doing verbal and mental exercises to help restore his brain function.

Once the mighty yacht captain of a large fleet, I sensed Peter had been the totalitarian captain at home too, fully in charge before his fated tumble. But Hara was clearly in charge now, since he became impaired. Peter didn't seem to like her bossing him around, restricting his freedoms, refusing him wine.

Peter stood up, angrily raising his voice, looking down on his shorter, cowering wife.

"Peter." I stepped in to intervene, gently interrupting him. "I feel uncomfortable when you talk to Hara like that."

Peter looked at me, surprised. "You do?"

"Yes." I looked at Hara, who appeared meek and grateful.

Peter sat down silently. His disheveled wife flew off to France after that, "to take care of property that had been damaged by a tornado," she said. So I had full charge of Peter's around-the-clock care.

After Hara left him with me, Peter said, "I am going to divorce her." He was considered mentally incompetent by his medical team, and incapable of caring for himself, but he didn't seem to notice or care.

"O.K, Peter," I said, "But for now, you need her."

He was silent. Maybe the truth was sinking in. Or maybe he was planning his escape.

* * *

I marveled at the beautiful ocean view one evening as we were finishing another decadent seafood dinner. "Wow, Peter, that view is just fabulous. I can't imagine a better view anywhere." But Peter wasn't impressed. He turned to me and said, "My place is better. This is nothing. Wait until you see where I live. It's magical."

I smirked, thinking he was just joking the way he always did. He was preparing to go back to his own home in Ramona, California, now that his brain injury day-treatment was complete and Hara was back from France. I would be joining them in their newly converted Peter-proofed house.

"The upstairs bedroom is roped off to prevent another fall," Hara said with finality.

It wasn't clear whether that precaution was taken for his safety or hers.

As the three of us drove to Ramona, I was stunned at how far out their property was, wondering if we'd ever reach it. We seemed to climb higher and higher into the cloudless sky in my stuffed car, turning this way, then that, past a herd of grazing black cattle, past the burnt-out millionaire estates from past wildfires, high up into the mountains we drove.

Then I saw it. As if the Solana Beach condo were a mere doll house, this customized castle was of monumental proportions on the tippy-top of the highest peak with a three hundred and sixty degree aerial view of Ramona and a clear vista all the way to the Pacific horizon.

The driveway alone was an impressive brick mosaic. A one level, attached guest house was where Hara wanted Peter to stay, since it didn't have any steps. The big house had an elevator near the kitchen pantry that went down to the six-car garage. Outside were several patios, landscaped terraces, and an orchard of ripening citrus trees that cascaded down the lush, irrigated hill.

We toured the spacious house and I saw the infamous marble staircase that swirled up to the second story. *He was lucky to have survived that fall.* Hara had constructed a barricade to keep Peter from climbing the steps. I was to accompany him on his daily walks to avoid further falls. It also felt as if I would be a welcomed buffer for their crumbling thirty-year marriage.

Peter explained that he had designed and built his elaborate home for his beloved wife in their early years together. I imagined them when they were young, a happy couple in love and wealthy, with all their hopes and dreams intact.

The furnishings were sparse, making the living room look sterile and hollow, with an eerie echo that gave it an empty, haunted feel. Hara's squeaky tennis shoes romped around upstairs reverberating through the whole house, while Peter sat in the living room with his scruffy Boston terrier on his lap, going numb in front of the TV. This was an amazing display of opulence, yet it felt so cold.

Who died here? Then I realized. *Oh, their marriage did.*

The day Peter drank that last Merlot and swore he could manage the staircase, I envisioned his wife begging him not to have another drink. He probably brushed her aside, dismissing her concerns, and then suddenly fell, crashing down and tumbling over himself to the bottom of the stairs. There he stopped with a dead thump, a pool of oozing blood spreading out from his head into Hara's desperate hands. She screamed for the gardener. It was the Mexican groundskeeper who rushed them to the hospital.

I sensed the deep loneliness they both felt, the vast space between them and how this immense house facilitated that distance, she upstairs, he down, separate beds, she on her endless international phone calls in the six languages she spoke. Yet none of them spoke to her husband.

And Peter alone, staring blankly at that obnoxiously loud TV, as it repetitively flashed stupid commercials. Dozing off and on, Peter snoozed to CNN with me, his nonpolitical daytime shadow. I felt no envy of their wealth, only pity for them. In this affluent house they built, the famed newlyweds became this older, estranged couple. Once so worldly and accomplished, now *both* seemed hopelessly handicapped.

Foreclosure on the failed fortress was imminent. Their fortune had run out. I was told they needed to hire someone more affordable, so I was let go. But later I learned that Hara did a "dump and run," leaving Peter in a low-grade nursing home while she fled the country.

I wish I could have stayed in the quaint-by-comparison Solana Beach cliffs condo longer with my friend Peter, the debonair old English gent, who had manifested so many of his dreams. His life ended much like an old-time war ship. Even the mightiest vessels eventually rust out, blow up, or sink.

EVERY LAST DOLLAR

With every last dollar and a risky advance on my credit card, I opened a new sober living house in a quiet suburban neighborhood of San Diego on faith. I wanted to start a home where mothers could stay with their young children. It was a safe place where they could live after being in rehab for drug and alcohol addiction, then gradually reunite with their families in a supportive environment. I called it "Safe Transitions for Women." I set out to find the perfect rental house that would have four bedrooms and a pool. I didn't have a job because I had been laid off, and yet, without any income, I was able to rent a house.

When I moved into the spacious two-story house, I found the previous tenants had left behind a lot of nice furniture we could use; three television sets, a tall dining room table with four chairs, a pool table, and a porch swing. The house was amazing, with my newly-purchased beds and comfy brown suede living room sectional, a heated pool in the back, and a relaxing patio lounge area.

If the house lease wasn't enough of an unexpected

blessing, enthusiastic volunteers from local AA meetings showed up at my door to help out with donations, marketing, and hands-on work. They decorated the house, set up bunk beds, and helped me paint. Build it and they will come. Wow, they did.

Soon my first resident was knocking at my door. Darla, (not her real name) a pretty, petite brunette in her thirties, fell in love with the house, and moved right in. She had three grade-school children who lived with her husband. They slept over one at a time to visit her while she continued her aftercare. They enjoyed private time with their mother in a home without their siblings and without any other residents, except me.

Darla thrived in the structured environment and her kids loved the pool. She had all of my attention. We talked for hours, as I mostly listened to the losses and traumas she had overcome to get sober.

After this client and I bonded, she shared her concerns about her troubled twelve-year marriage to a workaholic man. "My husband smokes pot and he could lose his job. He makes six figures and we could lose it all with one random drug test."

"Hmm, it sounds like he needs help, too."

Darla stayed with me for two months, attended AA meetings in the community, worked out at the local gym, and relaxed on an air mattress in the pool. She taught me how to eat vegetarian and I taught her how to stay sober. Her husband dated her, and had to be a gentleman, drug free, and treat her properly if he wanted her to go home. Darla said he was begging her to come home to him, but she wanted to stay longer.

"This is the first time in my life I can focus on *me*," Darla confided. "When I was a kid, it was my drug addicted parents, then men, and then my three children."

She had transformed herself from a strung-out soccer mom with her travel mug full of wine to nurse her hangovers, to a woman who carried around her recovery books and meditated on the patio, enjoying the scent of jasmine in the air and the hummingbirds at the feeder.

One evening we sat watching another episode of A & E's *Intervention* with a big bowl of popcorn between us.

"That girl reminds me of *me*," Darla said sadly, as we observed the actress on the screen yell at the caring family who were trying to save her life and get her into a rehab facility for her drug addiction. "My six year-old told me he got scared whenever I drank, because my voice would change."

Off alcohol and benzodiazepines, Darla now faced her life without her anesthetics. She had time to objectively view her role before she went home, and practice her self-care until it became a daily habit. She went to lots of AA meetings to get support for her sobriety.

When I wasn't nurturing Darla's recovery, or when she was away from the house, I was marketing the new enterprise. It wasn't enough, despite working fifteen hour work days. Some of the more established recovery homes in the area were shutting down due to the recession. So mine didn't really have a chance. It failed. I had to close it down quickly without enough capital to operate it.

I told Darla the sad news, but then I added, "If we did all of this so you could have a safe place to stay and get the one-on-one attention you deserve, then it was all worth it."

Darla cried tears of gratitude as we hugged good-bye and then she waved to me with a big grin from the car with her husband driving and three happy-looking kids in the back seat. They had their mom back. Darla was sober. I went bankrupt. We never saw each other again.

SINGING AT SEASIDE

I went to a Science of Mind or New Thought "church" to get help with my abundance thinking. I drove an hour and a half round trip to Seaside Center for Spiritual Living in Encinitas, California that teaches us that we create our own lives and experiences with our intentions, beliefs, and imagination.

I know this is true for me, so it has to be true for everyone.

As I was sitting in the teal-colored padded pews, I shot a desire into the air. *I want to sing on that stage.* This was in January and I knew absolutely no one there. I loved the vibe of the place and the jazz band was phenomenal. I could easily envision singing a solo up there at a Sunday service, behind all those leafy green trailing plants that graced the front of the wide, carpeted stage.

As time went on, I learned the congregational songs without much effort, thanks to the huge video screen, and I enjoyed the guest gospel artists. After some time had passed, I gave my business card to the Music Director, Reverend Fran, and said I would fill in or be a guest artist.

Little did I know that I would be singing there much sooner than I thought.

"I'm going on vacation," Reverend Fran said, "Can you sing here July fifteenth?"

Can I?

I smiled, "I'd love to." I started filling in when she needed time off. Soon she was struggling with chemotherapy treatments and needed more time away. I began singing weekly to a packed house of four hundred people for two services at nine and eleven. It just seemed so right that I was the one to do it. If not me, then who?

I enjoyed the Call to Worship song that started with, "*It is not I, but the Spirit within, that does these things I see before me.*" How true that is. I was making money doing the exact thing I loved, that I would have volunteered to do for free, at a leading edge new thought church that I had the utmost respect and love for. I even met one favorite author backstage, the renowned Terry Cole Whittaker. She signed my copy of her book, "Live Your Bliss," and mentioned my name on stage, thanking me for my song. *Cool.*

I introduced talented touring guest artists from around the world, (like Los Angeles), and shared the stage with them. I absorbed two wonderfully uplifting sermons every Sunday from the honorable Reverend Christian Sorensen, who lived what he taught.

This surely was a dream come true.

As I went out into the bright lights for a sound check, the full jazz band supporting me, and a sound guy telling me to sing a few lines for the mike check, it dawned on me that just a few months before I had been sitting in that audience, wishing I could be on this stage, and here I was, vibrating with anticipation that I could share my gift.

I substituted for the music director until she healed, (another miracle story.) We all prayed for her, and when she came back, it was easy for me to let go and step down. Our Reverend Fran, beloved pianist and dynamic vocalist, resumed her rightful place as the leader in front of the Seaside band. I had experienced my desire.

My intention had manifested and that was enough for me.

FAME ISN'T IT

When I put my human ego on the bottom shelf
And I'm closer to God than I am to myself
I can do great things
Even fly on angel's wings

A standing ovation!
A literary sensation?
Temporary elation
Still on the same station

It doesn't matter
If you love me or hate me
Praise me, or berate me
The audience, though stately
Won't take me home or date me

I leave with or without acclaim
Humbled, inside I'm still the same
It doesn't matter if you remember my name
Because real love is always better than fame.

JOSIE, THE WONDER CAT

Woo hoo! I finished graduate school in an accelerated eighteen months and I promised I would reward myself at the end of that grueling mental abuse with a new cat for company. I would have time to care for a pet now and I was ready for the responsibility, so I prayed for a new cat.

"God, you know what kind of cat would be good for me, please help me find one."

Within forty-eight hours my friend Joe, a San Diego jazz pianist, called me and said he knew a nice woman who needed a good home for her cat. She was moving into a new apartment with her daughter, to a complex that would not accept pets.

As a full time student and now an under-employed graduate, I didn't have any extra money to buy an animal. I went to the cat-owner's tiny, cluttered condo and saw this beautiful Russian Blue cat lying on her big four-poster bed like a princess. She was a lovely smoky gray ball of fur with yellow-green eyes that blinked at me serenely as I admired her.

The friendly fluff ball came up to me as I stood in the doorway.

"Wow," her owner said. "She never does that. She likes you."

"I already know I want her," I said, stroking her feathery-soft fuzzy head.

"Oh, good, I was so worried." The old woman looked relieved as she touched her heart. "I hate to let her go, but I can't keep her where I'm going. Her name is Fluffy."

"Hi, Fluffy," I said kneeling down to pet her long back. She flopped her whole body down with a thump on the beige carpet, arching in a long, luxurious stretch to maximize her massage.

This kind woman gifted me her beloved cat, actually thanking me for taking her off her hands. I received the cat I wanted, without any financial resources lost.

Additionally, the woman supplied a big bag of premium cat food, an automatic refillable water bowl and fancy food dish, and even a designer kitty litter box and pooper scooper. If that wasn't enough abundance, she also gave me a green shag-carpeted scratching post, colorful cat toys, and scoop-able, scented cat litter.

This amazing wonder cat was heaven-sent. We bonded instantly. She turned out to be the most wonderful, loving, low-maintenance cat I ever had. I named her Josie—after my friend Joe who found her for me. Thanks Joe and thanks God. I love her.

A TRANSFORMATIONAL MOVE

"God, what should I do now?" I was crying because I had just left the San Diego airport after dropping off my gorgeous adult daughter, Natalie, fresh out of college, and her doting boyfriend, Max. I was already missing them. I longed for one more kiss of Natalie's satiny sweet cheeks, the scent of her fruity shampooed brown hair, and see her deep Piscean blue eyes and cute rosebud lips.

They stayed with me over Christmas vacation. We'd had so much fun touring San Diego and biking together. I loved being with them.

Even though I was on a winter break from my fulltime counseling job, I felt empty, sad, and unfulfilled. I sat on my sunny balcony watching the sun on the trees twinkle, contemplating my now-lonelier life.

Then nature seemed to come alive all around me. The sky seemed to open up. The trees vibrated with their life force, their auras brightly flickering, as their branches pulsed with the wind. I heard the birds singing bolder than ever. The scent of my freshly watered hot pink geraniums sweetened my nose. A tiny hummingbird appeared before me, a significant sign of hope for me.

Instantly, a creative idea entered my mind.

I could sublet my high-rent, fully furnished apartment, collect a damage deposit, and use the money to fly back to my native Minnesota to visit my family—maybe even move back there if I wanted to. I didn't have to be without my tribe in California anymore.

So I said, "OK, God. I will put a rental ad on Craigslist and if you want me to go back to Minnesota, then let it rent out fast. If it does, that means I'm meant to go back there."

I placed the Internet ad, and within five minutes the phone rang.

"Hi, this is Morgan," an older woman's voice said. "I'm interested in your apartment. Can I come to see it tonight?"

I laughed, "Of course. I just placed the ad five minutes ago. You're the first caller. Can you wait two hours while I tidy up the place?" We agreed she would come at five thirty for the showing. I finished cleaning just before five and she called seconds later.

"I know I'm a little early, but I'm here, so can I see it now?" Since I had just finished picking up, I said sure.

We met at the locked gate where I showed her into the complex. She saw the little waterfall on the way in and looked relieved that the grounds were well-groomed.

"The last place I looked at was *awful,*" Morgan said.

We walked up to my second-floor apartment, and before we even entered my door, she smiled.

"I already know I want to take it."

I knew that she was the right renter the second I met her. Morgan told me she had her Ph.D. in psychology, the same field as my master's degree, and was a former Unity minister. I had sung professionally for the Science of Mind Church services every Sunday, so we had things in common.

She also said she flew in from Portland, Oregon, on "Spirit" airlines. That was the first time I ever heard of them.

We laughed at how uncanny it all was, and she said we were the answers to each other's prayers. She gave me the thousand-dollar deposit check that same evening, and I made flight arrangements to go back to Minnesota, knowing my California residence was now in good hands.

A CAT CARETAKER

I took my cat, Josie Bell, short for Josephine Belladonna, over to my cousin's house for a kitty play date with Rich's two older cats, Zephyr, who is blind and affectionate, and Pixel, who is skittish and doesn't like company. I was hoping against hope they might get along well enough for Rich to take care of my cat while I went to Minnesota to visit my family. Rich was understandably uneasy about Josie hissing at his precious felines. He said he didn't feel comfortable having my growly cat there. I was worried about anybody wanting to babysit my spoiled, anti-social cat. I loved her dearly and wanted her to be safe and happy in my absence.

I said to God, "You gave me a renter for my apartment. Now I need someone to take care of my cat." While outside carrying my laundry back up to my apartment, I noticed I had left the door open. Josie had snuck outside and stared at something high in the tree. I looked up and saw a fairy-like hummingbird, my sure spiritual sign that the kitty issue would somehow work out.

While quietly folding my laundry inside, I became

meditative and receptive. I got the inspiration to ask Morgan, the new renter, if she would mind caring for my cat if I took fifty dollars off her rent. Then Josie could stay in her own home, and Morgan would have some company. I called her before she moved in and asked if she would like to be a cat sitter.

"Oh yes," she said, "I've had cats before."

Problem solved.

STAN, THE CAR MAN

After leaving my car parked at my cousin's house in San Diego, I am skating indoors at my Minneapolis roller rink with my dear friend Colette. I flew in to Minnesota to visit my family and friends on vacation. I was even thinking about moving back. If I decide to stay, I will have to go get my vehicle in California and make the weary trek back, driving for three and a half days, two thousand miles, and stay at motels along the way, plus pay for all the gas.

I don't want to.

Stan, a friendly acquaintance at The Roller Garden in St. Louis Park, sat across from me at the square concession table, smiled broadly, and initiated a conversation. "I'm planning a trip to San Diego. I want to travel up the coast, rent a car, and then enjoy all the scenery on the drive back."

My mouth hung open. I couldn't believe what I just heard. I hadn't mentioned anything about my car to him or anyone at the roller rink. I was awestruck by his statement—a sudden, perfect answer to my unspoken need.

"You don't have to rent a car," I said, shaking my

head in disbelief. "My Toyota Corolla is still parked out there at my cousin's house, and I would love to get it back here to sell it to my son, Jeremy. You can drive it all week there and then drive it back if you want, and it won't cost you a thing."

"I would love to drive it back." Stan looked happy. He wouldn't have to rent a car. I wouldn't have to drive it back by myself.

I was extremely relieved, because I've made that West Coast trip to Minnesota three times already, and I wasn't up for another drive, especially in the winter.

I looked at Colette. "Do you see what's happening here? This is *God stuff.*" I was elated.

Colette smiled back at me. She was used to me talking to her about God and my miracles.

Stan did pick up my old car in San Diego, and drove it up the coast for his vacation, then all the way back to Minnesota for me. I never had to look for help with this predicament. It simply took care of itself. The solution even found me at the roller rink, where I felt right at home on skates. God knew my need and fulfilled it before I even asked, before I even concerned myself with it.

My adult son, Jeremy, bought this reliable old

Corolla with a few paint chips missing on the front bumper, and was able to look for and accept a new position as a delivery driver—an independent job he liked. With his new wheels, he was able to quit his pizza-making job he had hated for several years.

This win-win-win scenario is what God is famous for. If it helps everyone involved, then you know God is at work.

THE RED JAGUAR

I always thought that owning a Mercedes, a BMW, or a posh Jaguar was out of my reach. I thought I'd have to upgrade my psychology degree to an MBA or marry a rich guy to own such a beauty. My old war-torn but dependable Toyota needed replacing. I had just turned fifty and earned my master's degree so I thought *I deserve a new car.*

The only problem was I was broke, in debt, and unemployed. My credit card company didn't know that, or maybe they did, and sent me a blank check for a car loan so I could get into even more trouble. Their loan check was only accepted by a few select car dealerships. I didn't know which ones.

I went to the Toyota car lot and scanned the pre-owned vehicles for reliable Corollas in my price range, hoping to find one that was red or aqua, so I could spot it in large parking lots—something that would stand out in the bland sea of gray, black, and white cars. They had a slightly used aqua Corolla I liked, so I sat in the driver's seat. The eager young salesman dropped into the passenger seat next to me.

"It smells a little smoky," I said. I wrinkled my nose. I imagined he did too after he heard that, since the musty odor might cost him a sale.

We took it for a test drive anyway. The gray cloth seats were worn and slightly stained, but it was under fourteen thousand. I agreed to buy it "as is—no warranty." I wasn't enamored, but it was adequate, practical, and a fair deal—a marriage of convenience.

I filled out the financial paperwork with a nervous stomach, crossing my fingers, hoping they would accept my loan check for payment.

"It will be about half an hour to run your credit check," the salesman said.

"Okay."

I thought I'd drive around while I waited. That's when I spotted the Jaguar dealership next door. Something inside me said go take a look. How can it hurt to just drive around in there? So I cruised around the dealer parking lot to fantasize as I ogled the shiny Jaguars that boggled my mind. I knew I couldn't afford any of them—too expensive—and besides, I already found a used Toyota I was buying.

"Oh my God, that's my dream car." I said out loud

as I drove over to a stand-out scarlet Jag, a 2007 X-type sedan with a sun roof, chrome wheels, and the sleek curvy design I longed for. I parked my chipped economy car, walked to the luxury car, and peered inside, "Oh, wow, cream leather seats—my favorite."

I was in love.

I looked at the sticker, expecting to see an outrageous price, but it was only seventeen thousand. It looked in mint condition. No one came out to pressure me. I went inside the dealership and asked the young sales guy in a tailored suit about the car.

"Why is that Jaguar $17,000?" I asked.

"It was a dealer's car, but it's reached its expiration date. In fact, it just went down today to $13,900."

"Are you kidding?" I got flush, feeling like I just won something big. Swooning in serendipity, I felt like swirling in circles.

"It's right here on my daily report," the salesman said, pointing to a paper on his desk.

It was cheaper than the smelly Toyota next store. My heart jumped. I had to drive that Jaguar. We test drove it on the freeway. It was so fast and responsive, almost intuitive to my needs, plus it smelled like a new car. It was winter in Minnesota and it had four wheel drive and a killer heater. I was smitten all the way to my mittens. The seats even had bun-warmers to toast my cold bottom. Now overtaken by this stylish creampuff on wheels, I had to have it.

This car was made for me.

"Do you accept loan checks from this credit card company?" I handed him my check and took a deep breath, expecting it to be rejected on the spot.

"Let me see. . ." He took the check to his financial manager, who was on his phone and nodded yes from his glass office.

I couldn't believe it. A Jaguar—a *red* Jaguar—in my price range? Wow!

But I have a deal going on next door.

I didn't want to disappoint the Corolla salesman, but I wasn't going to buy that mediocre vehicle now—geez, it didn't even have floor mats. I drove back to the Toyota dealership to cancel the deal, dreading the confrontation I expected.

The Toyota salesman met me at the door and solemnly said, "Your credit was denied. I'm sorry."

Hallelujah!

I turned around and swaggered back to the Jaguar lot, and signed that miraculous check to purchase the best car I've ever had. Driving that Jaguar made me feel like a newly-crowned queen with her royal chariot.

Something prompted me to go look at that car. I think God wanted me to have it. People told me I would have problems with it, but the biggest problem I've had is that I can't seem to keep it clean enough.

Once after a car wash, I was driving down the road, belting out a tune, my head bopping under the open sun roof. A handsome young fellow passed me slowly, obviously flirting with me, and yelled out his window with a big smile, "You are *cool*!"

With that thumbs-up, I *felt* cool. Slick cars can do that to people, especially a red Jaguar from God.

DAVE'S DECISION

After being on a free online dating service called Ok-Cupid, I met Dave in February. We hit it off as a 97% match. He announced via e-mail that he was taking a business trip the following week.

"Where are you going?"

"San Diego."

How uncanny, I thought, since I had just flown in from there. My cat still lived there with Morgan in my San Diego sublet. I e-mailed, "Would you please do me a huge favor, Dave, and fly my cat back with you?"

"That is the most creative pick-up line I've ever heard," Dave wrote back.

My temporary tenant was moving out of my old apartment April first and I had to go back and pack up all my furniture and belongings because my lease was up. Morgan said she would keep the cat until she moved out. I was planning to move back to Minnesota to be near my family. I had been looking at flights to California and they were three hundred and fifty dollars, but suddenly it was spring break and they shot up to nine hundred. I didn't have the money and I needed to get back to San Diego.

After Dave and I had been on seven wonderful dates, he said he was going back to San Diego again the first week of April on another business trip, the very same week that I needed to clear out my place.

"I hope you won't mind, but I booked us a flight. I have a ton of frequent flier miles to use up. We also have a company-sponsored hotel room, a rental car, and an expense account for meals for both of us."

"What? Oh my God. . . Really? Wow. Thank you." It felt like the sky had opened up with abundant blessings.

Dave also had free luggage privileges and he politely offered to bring back an additional suitcase for me. He said he would stay a week longer to do some ADD testing at a special clinic. I would be able to bring Josie back myself. All I had to pay for was her pet carrier and cat fare. It was too good to be true. Yet, everything happened right on cue. Perfect timing.

* * *

Dave became my springtime Santa Claus. I went to a psychic to get some direction on my new career path in Minnesota and find out if my beloved Dave was The One.

"He is good for twenty years," Ruth, the psychic said. "Your heart is in Cali. I want to see you buy property there. He is as good as it gets. He doesn't know what to make of you. He likes you. He can get you into his company. They like couples. You will do a lot of traveling. You are an e*mpath*. You take on other people's feelings. He will help you buy property." Ruth, the sleuth, said all this about Dave, I presumed. "I see you in a red suit speaking to a group of CEO's in Germany."

Germany! Where Dave just was, on his last business trip before he went to San Diego! We did an angel card reading and my true love card came up twice. Why twice, and why was there depression and anxiety in between those two cards? Hmmm…

Here I was sitting in so-called sun in a north-facing atrium at the Chanhassen library, recalling my psychic reading, when Dave called from my apartment in San Diego. He took photos of my furniture for sale. It's like we traded places. It felt so odd. I didn't tell Dave what the psychic said because I didn't want to scare him, or that I could *feel* his energy a second or two before he calls me. t

I ought to write a book about my manifestations. It

appears that I receive everything I need all the time. Not sure how, but I know faith, gratitude, awareness of God's blessings and love, prayer and meditation all make me receptive. I think Dave senses this. He said that he told his friends I am "very spiritual." That was the day he went to get his oil changed and I went with him. Our two car dealerships just happened to be next door to each other. Crazy fate. His dealership was the same one that had turned me down. I got my Jaguar washed for free at my swanky dealership next door. And it had better coffee.

Things seemed to be going so well. Too well. Dave asked me if I would be exclusive with him. I said yes. After we fooled around and I fell in love with him, he told me how good it was, that he "fell hard and fast" for me. Then he turned to me in his car a few days later.

"What if we're just *friends*?"

Huh? I should have run from him right then, but my licentious legs wouldn't move. I looked up in disbelief.

"You are *not* The One!" He said adamantly. "I don't see us in a long-term relationship."

But the psychic does . . . I heard his words. They came from his lips, but his eyes, voice, and body language were not saying that. I was not convinced.

He continued with hurt in his eyes, "I'm not ready."

That, I believed. His ex-wife Kimberly must have hurt him in some fundamental way, so now I was paying for the "Sins of Kim." I was hurt. This was on top of losing my spacious, sunny apartment in San Diego, all my comfy furniture, and staying in a cool, dark basement in my friend's house in winter. My foretold future fiancé was backing out of our shared destiny. I was the right woman at the wrong time. An invisible spear jabbed my heart from the inside. Why had I left San Diego again?

Even though I'd lived in Minnesota most of my life, it did not feel like my home. I missed San Diego terribly. I'd made closer connections with my family, but now I felt alienated from *myself.* Suddenly Dave was a stranger, too.

"I can honestly say I don't know what I want," Dave admitted.

I felt pushed away. It hurt, but I still just sat there, paralyzed, and simply said, "God is my Source." I didn't budge from his car during our talk at the park even though I could have easily walked home. I still wanted him. Fiercely. I thought about our upcoming trip together to San Diego in a shared hotel room . . . with no sex? How was that going to work? Where would I find a *burka* to wear to bed with him?

* * *

In San Diego, Dave and I shared a platonic California king and said "Goodnight." No touching. We went to my spiritual center on Sunday and my old beau Michael was there with an early birthday gift for me, (his latest thrift store bargain) and handed it to me in front of Dave, (good public relations.) If that wasn't impressive, then Reverend Christian gave me an honorable mention from the stage, thanking me for being their interim soloist. I suddenly had celebrity status with Dave sitting beside me with his humungous hand on my leg.

He said we're just friends and then he kissed me on the lips, held my hand, hugged me tight. Such confusing mixed messages. I told Dave that I saw his blue aura and it didn't faze him at all. He actually seemed pleased.

As if all this weren't enough—us meeting, the timing of this all-expense paid trip he so generously gave me, I also had a buyer in San Diego for all the large furniture I couldn't take with me. It was the best, easiest sale there could possibly be—the future tenant of my apartment. He wanted everything. I didn't have to move one piece of heavy furniture. This saved money on movers since I didn't need any. Dave, my friends, and I packed up all the rest of my things into boxes that fit in a van, dropped it into storage, and would ship my lighter-weight clothing. I donated my precious plants to my pleased neighbors. It was a miracle how it all worked out.

After Dave brought me coffee in bed, I sat there feeling lost and lonely in our luxury hotel room while Dave did his ADD testing online for his emotional I.Q.

I pointed to my face and said, "*Sad*." I let my tears show. "I want to go home, but there's no home to go to."

He came over and hugged me, "I know you have one foot in both places." He sat, held me, and we cried.

That night we watched a surreal movie. It was called *God is the New Elvis* about a sexy back-up singer to Elvis. She turned into a celibate Reverend Mother in a convent. Her sad man-friend was completely in love with her and could not have sex with her. How ironic, as I laid there next to my beloved Dave, fully clothed like a nun myself, with a cold, stark mile between us in that giant bed.

"I don't think you're ready for a long-term relationship because you're not over your ex-wife yet."

He did not deny it.

* * *

I left Dave in lovely San Diego. He needed another week to finish his business there. My old apartment was cleaned out, my stuff was safely in storage, and my full suitcases were all I had as I made a new start in Minnesota.

I was back in cold, cloudy weather, sobbing because it felt like Dave broke up with me. I took a brisk walk-jog in the Chanhassen Park and leaned my back up against a tall pine tree to soak up its healing nature energy. I then refocused my grief to what I am grateful for, what's good in my life, and what I am looking forward to.

I got three e-mails from Dave reiterating that he just wanted to be my friend. *Ego-rrhea! OK, leave me alone then, Scaredy Cat!*

I cut the spiritual cord that tied my bloody heart to him, to emotionally individuate myself. Snip, snip. Yet I wanted to turn around and go right back to Cali. . .

It rains a lot here, and hardy Minnesotans always make the best of everything. They say, "We need the rain." Personally, I do not need this rain . . .

And I don't hear the Scandinavian accent anymore, which means I have it again. I couldn't believe Dave was gone after all he had given me. What haunted me most was the desirous *longing* in his eyes. Was it just lust?

When Dave dropped off my other suitcase a week later, he said self-centeredly, “I wonder how much more successful I would have been if I’d treated my ADD sooner.”

“Why? So you could be as gray as Obama?”

We laughed and he asked for a hug. I gave him one like it was our last. I see now that my behavior towards Dave was skewed because of what the psychic told me. I treated him like my future husband when I was just an acquaintance to him. I felt even more lost after that reading. Was she talking about someone else? I was so confused and anxious. I needed a job desperately. I craved sweets. I wanted to eat the roof off the house.

I wondered how long I’d be in Minnesota this time. It never felt permanent, but it did feel important that I was there. I downed a cantaloupe and obsessed over popcorn. I got drunk on sugared peaches. My gut was full and on fire and still I felt empty. I was only 1% more sure that I should be here than in Cali—not a landslide decision.

I started a new job and then called Dave and told him they had me stationed at one of their many group homes—located right across the street from his condo! What were the chances? He was home convalescing after his knee surgery. I wasn't stalking him—really—it was serendipity again, that sneaky Law of Attraction.

"Do you need anything?" I asked, doting on him.

"No," he said, "Becky is taking good care of me."

Becky? His new girlfriend? I was in shock. That explained it. And it was over, just like that. We haven't spoken since.

POETIC LESSON

I loved a big dude named Dave

Who got scared and ran to his cave

The psychic predicted

We'd both be addicted

But I guess he just wasn't that brave!

* * *

My San Diego apartment was gone along with all of my possessions. I couldn't get licensed in Minnesota with my California credentials in counseling. I thought we were destined to be a couple after all these miracles, but he left.

After staying in chilly Minnesota for five cloudy months, I was ready to go back to sunny San Diego. This again meant another painful separation from my family. I packed up my Jaguar on May 20th for my long drive back to California; now homeless, broke, and jobless, to start all over in San Diego for the *fourth* time.

Grief Won

I ran from Grief as it stalked and surrounded
Winded and wounded, my bludgeoned heart pounded
That relentless hunter poked its blunt rifle tip
Frisked me, then cuffed me, in its grievous grip

I hid from Grief as it viciously sought me
Then I ran, panting, determined to flee
No matter where I went, it followed - how odd
Seething, I'm ambushed by its firing squad

Cornered and aching, I sought quick relief
Sharp and pointed its aim, heart-targeted Grief
Distractions don't work, I tried that too
Compulsive addictions only grew

When I tried to rise above defeat
It slammed my face to the concrete

Now on top, Grief hovered and hissed;
"Your ego has no place in this!"

Asthmatic, heavy lungs and chest
Hold tears that had been put to rest
Ruptures now, what was repressed
The volcano bursts, I face the test

No way to avoid my mirror meeting
Surrendered, I gave up, totally beaten
Engulfed in piercing pain, whimpering and weeping
Helpless now, Grief took pity, stopped creeping

I held it tight as it wrestled and wriggled
To get itself free (I think it even giggled)
Exhausted, I let go. Then away from me it sped
Like darkness at daybreak, Grief finally fled.

The Most Dreaded Disease

Is this the woe of a writer, an artist's angst?
That jokester, depression, playing its pranks?
The lonely longing for a lost lover's lure
A lingering conclusion that has no cure?

The needling that maybe I can't hack it
Vibrates inside this old straitjacket
Immobilized by creeping doubt
Too struck with fright to even shout

The trap of discontentment, deep in its clutches
Broken hopes, tangled nerves, without any crutches
Death wish jaunts from a whispering devil's taunts
Failures past, current pressures, a nearer future haunts

My mind, all crumpled, cowers in its crevice
Ducking, it screams, "Don't let the ghosts get us!"
On humbled knees, I'm begging God please
Take away my fear, the most dreaded disease.

THE MIRACLE HOUSE

I drove my completely crammed Jaguar from Minneapolis to the West Coast across the desert in 116 degrees, feeling like *Jaynes Bond.* Brave and bold, yet also afraid my tires might melt off or blow out and I'd be dusted along the side of the dead-smelling highway.

With more faith than funds, I left with a vague opportunity to share an apartment near enchanting Mission Bay, right where I wanted to be, with Nora, an acquaintance. Her invitation inspired me to leave Minnesota where I couldn't find even a "B" job because my professional certifications wouldn't transfer states. I gave her my deposit check, and we waited for our move-in date.

While I was waiting, I stayed with my generous musician friend Joe, in his little one-bedroom cottage in La Mesa. With the lower half of my body in his tiny living room, and my head, as usual, in the dining room, I slept on a stiff futon pad in the hallway between rooms, a fitting metaphor for my transitional status. My lovely cat, Josie, was with me. I was unemployed, and it was a free place, so I didn't complain, not one bit, at least not out loud.

About a week before the big move-in date, Nora called me up, very angry about my asking routine questions of the resident manager about the apartment, as if I had no rights as a future tenant or her housemate. She yelled at me based on misinformation she received from the front office. Finally, when she wasn't getting the cowering response she wanted from me, she shouted, "This isn't going to work out. I'm giving you your deposit back."

I felt relieved. I thanked God for showing me that side of her *before* we moved into the apartment.

Now where was I going to live?

Rents are high in San Diego, and housing isn't easy to find, especially without a job. Then Joe announced he was going to move up to Santa Cruz to be with a woman he just met up there. We discussed me renting his cheap little house, taking over his payments when he left, so I was hopeful about that possibility.

Then a week later he announced he wasn't going to move, he was just going to visit her. It made more sense, but where did that leave me? We were starting to get on each other's nerves like any rambling late night codger-music man trying to live with a chirpy morning chanter.

"Please don't sing..." Joe winced painfully, his eyelids half-mast at eight o'clock in the morning.

We were both sleep deprived, crowded, and irritable. I decided I needed space, privacy, and real rest, so I went to sleep in my leather-lined Jag, a welcome retreat from the tenement of testosterone.

I was virtually homeless for two whole nights, and if anyone would have asked me where I was staying, I would have truthfully replied, "The Hilton Hotel on Mission Bay." I was honestly sleeping there—*in their parking lot*—in my Jaguar with the expired Minnesota license plates I couldn't afford stickers for. Hyper-vigilant, I was constantly on the lookout for California Highway Patrol and police squad cars like a notorious outlaw.

My first homeless evening was spent scraping and scrubbing the neon orange stains off my car hood from the gluttonous bandit seagulls that ate someone's Hot Cheetos.

I actually slept better there than I did at Joe's house, as a scruffy car-bound transient with the intoxicating scent of Jasmine, a refreshing bay breeze from my open moon roof, the night sounds of soothing cricket-friends, and the blazing fireworks show that crackled from SeaWorld. I was all alone in my star-speckled, vagabond world. I loved my freedom, until it was time to pee.

No one saw me make my clandestine three a.m. jaunt to the park potty, my guilty face aptly disguised in my teal hoodie, with a stuffed pocket full of Kleenex because The City of San Diego is too cheap to pay for all that elite public toilet paper. I called it *papel de toilette publique.* It's prettier.

The second night was my last homeless night, thanks to my skater-friend DJ Dave, who asked me if I'd housesit for his deceased parent's estate. I could barter my organizing, cleaning, and gardening skills for free housing. It was a big place, I could live there alone, and it wouldn't cost me a thing, utilities included. Did I mention I had been wishing for a paid-for house with fruit trees so I would be unencumbered to write a book about my life?

My prayer was answered.

B.E.D. RECOVERY

I couldn't believe it. I found myself bottomed out with a Binge Eating Disorder (B.E.D.) Calling it BED for short is appropriate, since I often took food to bed with me. Food was my lover, my best friend. I depended on it to get me through uncomfortable feelings. I used it to numb out. It started out innocently, reaching for just a little more food for comfort, but it grew into a vicious habit, a monster I lost control of. In fact, I needed real help.

I wasn't obese, so how could it be that serious? I didn't throw up like a person with bulimia, or restrict my intake like I was anorexic. I didn't eat a whole gallon of ice cream like the binge eaters I read about, so it was easy to think I was normal. Yet I still wanted to eat from morning until night, grazing mindlessly as my meals had fuzzy beginnings and virtually no end. I was a binge-eater, a grazer, a midnight muncher.

To make matters worse, my life was in chaos.

When I had moved from sunny California to the dead dark winter of Minnesota to be near my family, I was unemployed, anxiously job searching on my computer all day, with a fully stocked refrigerator nearby for consolation.

I had also been suddenly left by Dave, the man I was in love with. I believed he would be my life partner, at least that's what a psychic said. I created an idealized image of us being together. Imagine my shock when my dream of us died and I had been quickly replaced. *Ouch!*

Grief hit hard. Maybe it's cumulative if you add Mark to the mix and all the other men, plus no family around for support. I was always the one who left, but now I had been left, unexpectedly. My heart felt bludgeoned. Betrayed, humiliated, and abandoned, I cried a lot. But more than that, I ate a lot. I ate until I felt sick.

It was my not-so-little secret that I ate so much and so often. My housemate, Jean in Chanhassen, didn't know how much I was eating on the side, nor did my mother, who thoughtfully gave me much of the free food I binged on. I had snacks stashed in my bedroom so it was available to me any time, even at one o'clock in the morning.

I suffered from digestive problems. I thought it was normal from eating a mostly vegetarian diet. I thought nothing of the fact that I grazed most of the day. Crunchy unsalted peanuts, syrupy canned peaches, crumbly scones,

McDonald's hot fudge sundaes, and large bowls of microwave popcorn. Supposedly "guilt-free" potato chips and dark chocolate were my panacea. Anything I could chew on auto pilot was devoured. Most of it was "natural," so what was the problem?

There were a lot of problems. First, I had trouble sleeping because my busy stomach was rumbling all night with my bedtime fare and subsequent midnight snacks. The food I ate so late energized me when my body was supposed to be shut down for the night. During the day I fell victim to beckoning fast-food drive-through restaurants as if they were my salvation. I chomped on greasy burgers on fluffy white buns, crispy fries in trans-fats, and lover-like ice cream shakes, spending time with food in my car like they were secret friends of mine.

Like a hypocrite, I acted like an uppity food snob in front of my family and friends, declining their luscious homemade desserts, because I knew I didn't have control. I feared buffets, potlucks, and holiday dinners because I knew that once I started, I might not be able to stop my insatiable craving for more, more, ***MORE.***

After spiritual services one Sunday, there were three different cake offerings—vanilla, chocolate, and carrot cake. I couldn't decide, so I had all three. I was ashamed of my lack of self-discipline. It felt like a constant battle between me and the food. I bought a large watermelon, chilled it, cut it in half, and went after it with a big spoon—justifying it as mostly water.

After I finished overeating that, still unsatisfied, my mind would yell, "What can I eat *next*?" Like a wild animal frantically hunting for new prey, I opened the cupboards for my magic fix, then the refrigerator door, expecting to see some kind of delicious answer to my emotional hunger.

Nothing worked.

Sugar only satiated my brooding brain temporarily. Binge behavior might not seem like such a strange thing by itself, but I didn't stop there. I went on to gorge on popcorn, or a *whole bag* of potato chips. Chocolate chip trail mix disappeared in minutes, muddying my hands, face, steering wheel and, most of all, my mind.

Even though I saw what I was doing and wanted to stop, I couldn't. It was this perplexing loss of control that scared me the most.

When I received a large bag of mixed Halloween candy last year, I was told by my date, "You better not eat it all." He was half-kidding.

Offended, I promised, but I ended up eating all the full-sized candy bars myself, alone, and they were far from being my favorite. I was consumed by a frenetic, driven need to fill my emptiness. Once my sweet tooth was triggered, it was on. Running ravenous, I became addicted to anything with processed sugar.

I didn't grieve the deeply felt disappointment and tremendous loss of the man I loved in Minnesota. Instead, I ate over it.

I got high on food, numb, foggy-headed, buzzed. I gained a lot of weight in a short time. But that didn't even bother me that much. What really struck me was how out of control I was. My behavior was disordered around food—lying about it, hiding it, overeating it, obsessing over it. I showed people the healthy eater I wanted to be, when in fact I was still bingeing on the fast food I detested—when no one was around. It was my sick way of coping with constant anxiety, depression, overwhelming fear, anger, and intense grief.

My eating disorder greeted me first thing in the morning and again, especially, at night, when the cupboards coaxed, "I'll help you sleep and make everything all right." Its siren song seduced me all afternoon from the jiving jukebox-fridge: "I'm here for you, baby. Come and get me, you'll feel better." It lied. Giving in only made me feel worse.

I remember being four years old, searching my neighborhood in the early morning for companions, with my sticky little hands gripping my box of Cap'n Crunch cereal. An anxious kid, I bought orange popsicles for my younger cousins and ate three to their one. I often finished the cafeteria trays of my classmates, and once downed a dozen oranges when I was mad at my dad. When I told an adult I ate them all, he said, "That could give you kidney problems, honey."

Now I'm allergic to citrus. I guess my body finally said, "Enough!"

Even after attending Overeaters Anonymous (OA) meetings, I still couldn't get off the sugar entirely. I kept giving in on a whim. I tried to control it. I achieved clean eating for a few days, but I could never hold it together for long. I kept swearing off sugar and then relapsing.

What was wrong with me?

I knew I was in rough shape when I went out for an ice cream cone that I had sworn off earlier, and then immediately wanted to go through the line for another one.

My friend Bob said, "One bite is too many and a thousand is never enough." He was right. Twice I put together thirty days of abstinence from sugar. Then I blew it. I finally surrendered, admitted total defeat, and asked God for help. I was finally ready to do whatever it took.

"How can this happen?" I complained to my new OA sponsor. I felt like I was on my knees, begging God fto relieve me of these cravings and obsessions. If my sugar addiction was activated, the stop switch in my brain didn't work, like an amped-up appetite gone haywire. I had to admit I was not normal when it came to certain foods, much like booze to an alcoholic.

For a month I attended OA meetings every day, like an outpatient treatment program. I saw people getting well. The first week of my new eating structure was torture—three distinct, planned meals a day—with *nothing* in between. No snacks. No little treats. In OA they say "three meals with *life* in between." I changed it to fit my own difficult withdrawal, "Three meals a day with *tears* in between."

You can't imagine how hard it was to have that basic order established. It seems so simple now, but at the time I was in bed, sometimes crying without my habitual grazing behaviors to defend me from sadness and loss. As emotionally raw as I felt, I committed to myself, "I will stick to this moderate, nutritious eating plan *no matter what!"* Then I held on tight to my abstinence from sugar.

I had moved back to San Diego after, pardon the pun, a fruitless job search in Minnesota. So I was missing my family. But now I had support from recovering compulsive overeaters like me. These people understood me. I was open and honest with them and I felt better.

I humbly prayed to God for the strength to overcome my problem. As I drove over the city's hill on Interstate Eight heading west to an OA meeting in Mission Valley, my consciousness was somehow lifted above everything, into a higher perspective.

From this sky-view, I peered down at the multitude of profiting fast-food chains, their chimneys spewing greasy-smelling smoke into the air to attract customers. I saw how expensive, unhealthy, and addictive this so-called food was. I saw giant billboards pushing poison on fast-food junkies in exchange for their lunch money.

I saw the empty calories, the disregard for public health, and all the resulting obesity, the cravings for sugar, grease, and salt—how physically toxic it all was. I suddenly lost my appetite. After praying for God's help, my lifelong *need* to overeat vanished.

Growing organic greens in my backyard, I prepared my fresh meals at home. I did research on super-foods and experimented with how my body and brain felt after eating high-quality raw food. I took my own meal in my cooler when I went out, so I wouldn't need to stop for convenience. This spiritual awakening healed me from self-indulgence and self-deception. I wanted to do what God intended, to eat only the best foods to fuel my body.

I went to an OA *maintainers* meeting. They said you needed six months of abstinence, and to be in a medically sound weight range, before you could speak at the podium. I made a commitment to be six months abstinent from sugar so I could speak at that meeting. They announced that newcomers should not donate any money, but could buy literature instead. I had exactly eleven dollars to buy their Twelve Step Workbook. I reached for it like a life preserver.

At that meeting, I met a slim gal who said she had attended ninety meetings in ninety days. She was my hero. I felt an inner nudge to get up and ask her to be my

Sponsor, like a divine reflex. As instructed, I texted her exactly what I ate for my three moderate meals each day to keep me honest, aware, and accountable. I was ready to tackle this issue head-on, mouth closed.

My saliva glands were still on overdrive with no snacks to appease them. In other words, *I drooled.* Waiting to eat my next scheduled meal, all my grief I had stuffed down came bubbling back up like a hot spring. I joked to my O.A. group, "My tears are just my fat melting out of my eyeballs." I hurt all over. My comfort foods and sweets were gone and I had to weigh and measure my healthy servings to appropriate portions, not overindulge. I was not to eat for mere pleasure, comfort, social recreation, or solitary entertainment.

"What?" I railed against normal portions, "Only *half* a cup of brown rice or mashed potatoes? Are you kidding me?" I used my new measuring cups for accuracy since I had no sense of what a serving size was.

Quantity reduction and my new three-meal-a-day regimen created precise order where previously there had been none. It seems crazy now, but this was quite a terrifying prospect at the time, as if my detox off sugar, and no grazing, would somehow crush me into a million pieces. It wasn't just food choices, portions, or the timing of meals, but my undisciplined eating *behaviors* as well. Now I made myself sit down at the dining room table, put everything aside, and eat mindfully, with gratitude. Previously I ate while I multi-tasked at my computer, by the stove, over the sink, lying down, at the counter, walking around, while cleaning up, even in the bathroom. Now I ate my balanced, measured, sit-down meals at the kitchen table like a civilized guest.

I enjoyed every delicious bite and when my meal was over, it was *over*. No more food until the next meal. (What a concept.) I drank decaf coffee or tea, and a lot of iced water. This fullness helped me get through to my next meal. I refused to eat *anything* between meals. I needed to reprogram my body and mind to wait. My stomach felt unusual—authentic hunger pangs? I hadn't let myself get hungry before. I got a normal rhythm going with mealtimes and I felt so much better. The pounds melted off easily and quickly with abstinence from sugar, junk, and excess. My body got exactly what it needed nutritionally—no more, no less—like premium fuel. As a *health-atarian*, I said goodbye to recreational sugar and white flour. I embraced fresh fruit as my daily desserts.

At some point I quit opening the refrigerator out of habit, stopped wandering in the kitchen uninvited, gave up searching cupboards for imaginary goodies. With my feelings intensified, I had tea with them, wrote in my journal, called recovery friends, and shared my struggles at meetings with people who understood. I worked all the tools OA offered and took all twelve steps they suggested.

It was a rough few weeks of deep sadness. Then one morning I rejoiced over a normal morning constitution.

As each pound melted off, so did another layer of sadness, revealing a more serene me. Surrendered and humbled, my big ego shrank. I thanked God for my recovery. It truly was a miracle. I became a vulnerable human being who needed to be fed by my Higher Power, fed by people who care, not a pineapple to the core.

When I reached my goal weight in about eighty days without exercise, people asked me in amazement, "How did you do it? What are you eating?"

I had one serving of each item from four food groups, including half a cup of a natural carbohydrate like oatmeal, brown rice, or mashed potatoes.

I felt balanced, satisfied, sane…dare I say, *ordered?*

Once sluggish and bloated, I was 175 pounds when I

started my abstinence from refined sugar. I surpassed my goal weight of 150 to be an unbelievable 140. I hadn't seen that number since high school. It's the first time in my life that I actually weigh less than the fib on my driver's license. What's better, I'm staying within a two pound range every month.

I had lost and gained the same yo-yo pounds a hundred times before this, vigorously working out at the gym or Jazzercise to compensate for over-indulging. Now I know it was the *extra* food and the *type* of food I ate, not a lack of exercise that kept me heavy. This time I had a plan I could live with for life. I gave it all to God.

Today I slide easily into my size-eight jeans, but more than that, I have order and peace. I value my body with fresh produce and proper nutrition. With a closer spiritual connection, my life has improved in every way. Fulfillment comes from being of service and order is a wonderful thing.

Clean, Green, Lean and Serene

No sugar, no meat
No dairy, no wheat
You ask: "What on earth
Does this woman eat?"

The most beautiful salads you ever saw
A colorful rainbow of veggies, raw
Fabulous fruits of every kind
Fresh of course, minus the rind

I wok exotic green stir fries
With attention to the portion size
I eat brown rice, oatmeal, and spuds
Eggs with onions and broccoli buds

Bean tostadas, hold the cheese
Soy-milk smoothies with bananas I freeze
Legume soups and lentil stews
Sunflower seeds, pecans, cashews

Since going on flat-ab alert
I eat my greens and skip dessert
Noticing now that more men flirt
Since I slid into my smaller skirt

I grow green beans in organic soil
I sauté them with garlic and olive oil
Tomatoes with basil, parsley, sage
We can look younger than our age

With an apple, mango, peach, and pear
Never worry about what to wear
When you let go of the extra load
Your body's in true fashion mode

I breathe better, my jeans fit great
I'm in good health, I'm at goal weight
With more energy, I concentrate
On a brand new me to celebrate!

ONE DOOR CLOSED, ONE OPENED

I dated Chad, a kind but grieving widower, for about three months when I realized my romantic and emotional needs were not getting met, and he had expressed his own concern about not being ready for a serious relationship. One night I awoke at 3:40 a.m. and that quiet voice within nudged me to go online, which I never do at that hour.

I logged onto Ok-Cupid, the internet dating site where Chad and I met. We had come up as a 99% match. I saw Chad was online. He was in cyberspace shopping for women in the middle of the night. Then I remembered the discrepancy between his age on his dating profile, 52, and reality, 56. Age, to me, didn't matter. I've dated men fourteen years older and quite a bit younger. It was this dishonesty that stood out for me and his offhand comment, "I struggle with feeling good enough." It made me feel that perhaps he's not for me.

My clairvoyant friend Karise was adamant that I break up with him immediately. I said I needed time to sleep on it first, and come up with a succinct sentence to end it with him.

I decided to let him go gently, and said I needed a man who is ready. What I really needed was honesty and integrity. I dealt with his loss by telling myself I was being true to myself and my ideals. No tears, no anger, just a steady resolve to stick with my principles and my goal of a loving, faithful marriage.

POETIC LESSON

I dated a widower named Chad

Who was always so droopy and sad

He lied about his age and height

On the internet dating site

So leaving him wasn't that bad.

That door was closed, so I opened my mind. I lay in bed one night envisioning what it would feel like to have a new man, holding my body in his arms, spooning me from behind, kissing me, being very affectionate while cuddling me, and me feeling completely loved, secure, and cherished. I could almost feel his big warm arms around me. It felt heavenly and I smiled and leaned back into my cozy romantic vision, savoring its sweetness.

Sunday morning I went to Unity Church as usual, feeling like a million bucks. A white-haired gentleman greeted me outside as I came in. I smiled broadly and said "Good morning." Then I took my usual seat in the second row. Within seconds, that tall white head sat in front of me, then looked back and smiled. He chatted with me like he was self-assured, and said that he had forgotten his leather jacket at a seminar there the Friday night before.

"Hi, I'm Ty." He had a twinkle in his attractive brown eyes, and his presence was so loud I couldn't tune into what he was saying. He spoke faster than an auctioneer at a used car lot. Next thing I knew he was asking me for my phone number. He was so confident, I gave it to him.

That afternoon he called and asked me out for coffee

that evening. We met at Starbucks and the only place to sit was in big leather arm chairs, across from a young African American couple. The contented woman sat comfortably on her lover's lap. We were obviously being watched by our audience as we met for our first date.

A Caucasian man in the other chair across from us looked impaired by alcohol. He felt compelled to comment on what he was witnessing, "Are you two married? No? You look great together—like you're a couple."

I joked, "Well, he does have sexy hands," I said, and took his hand in mine like I was going to read his palm, then whispered in his ear, "I can't read palms."

The drunken man slurred, "Geez, I'm getting horny just watching you two."

This was embarrassing to hear on a first date, from an obviously intoxicated observer.

He also blurted, unprovoked, "You two are going to go everywhere."

I turned to Ty smiling and said half-kidding, half not, "Italy?"

We were amused being the center of attention in our little sitting room of spectators. I realized they had been waiting to see who would show up in my seat.

"She's a princess," the man slurred, with foam forming around his lips.

"I think she is more like a *queen*…wiser," Ty said, looking for my reaction.

I winked at him, admiring his eloquence and carbonated personality, with that knowing look like we had our own little secret between us now—or at least we both had sobriety.

This successful first date led to another date the next day with a nice healthy restaurant lunch and a romantic walk along Mission Bay, San Diego, a place I have spent a lot of time at, and love. We had fun like little kids, swinging on the swings at the park, walking silly on top of a brick wall, holding hands seductively along the shore. He wrapped me in his blanket like a canopy and kissed me underneath it.

Then Ty took my hand and we headed to the Hilton Hotel where we laid down on a cushioned double lounger on the private patio of a guest room. It looked unoccupied. We were like devious teenagers with nowhere to make out. Ty put his arms around me, and I suddenly felt that familiar feeling I'd had in my vision.

I told him, "I just fantasized last night about a man

spooning me from behind and how good it felt."

Upon hearing that, he readjusted himself more behind me and wrapped me in a warm embrace that made me melt into him. My vision came to life in an instant.

Here he is. I was giddy that my manifestation had arrived so fast. Ask and ye shall receive. . .

Just then a loud banging jolted us as we looked up and saw an angry guest inside the sliding glass door gesturing for us to leave his patio. We sat up, got off his lounger, apologized, and ran giggling.

* * *

As time went on with dating, I sensed that Ty just wasn't ready for any kind of real commitment. We fooled around at his house a little, but we didn't actually go out anywhere after the initial "getting to know you" three dates.

Ty, looking attractive and alert, said from his bed, "I want to make love with you."

"I'm waiting for marriage to have sexual intercourse," I replied. I had learned my lessons well.

He quit calling after that, as I suspected he would. He seemed like the poster playboy for "emotionally unavailable," or "commitment-phobic." I wasn't going to be used ever again.

Ty texted me two weeks later on Valentine's Day, testing my resolve perhaps, or just being sentimental.

I read his text on February fourteenth: "Do we have any unfinished conversation between us?"

I laughed and texted him back. "Since most of our communication was nonverbal, I thought we both found resolution."

POETIC LESSON

I dated a tall guy named Ty

Five seventeen inches high

He chased me down at church

Then left me in the lurch

Not a "marital sex" kind of guy!

A GENTLEMAN WILL WAIT

I'm a strong woman who's been on the road
I've learned to pass up the occasional toad
He needs to learn a woman has a will
For holding out for someone better still
Tell it to him kind, but straight:
"A gentleman will wait."

It's the frisky ones who've failed before
Who grope and push and ask for more
The ones who can't take "Maybe"
Who don't know how to treat a lady
A wise man knows to follow fate
A gentleman will wait

They want to walk you to your car
Even when it isn't parked that far
They'll try to kiss you at your door
But I've been through all this before

Don't get me wrong, I love good men
But there's a time and a place
For what and when
Avoid the prelude at the gate
A gentleman will wait

You've been to that party or that dance
And that guy who's looking for romance
Is thinking he might have a chance
To win you with words or a hopeful glance
He'll try before it gets too late
But a gentleman will wait

So take some of my sage advice
It doesn't help to be too nice
Tell him no quickly, and be firm
Leave him with no uncertain terms
He's not the kind of man to date
A gentleman will wait.

HOW FOOD CAME

I was completely broke. I had been to meetings for debtors who wanted to stop using debt, so I had cut up my credit cards. I told a friend that I used up the rest of my food budget to buy two pairs of pants that fit my new, slimmer body. I really wanted those pants. I needed them. I said to my friend Karise, “I like rice and beans. It’s OK.”

I went to a staff meeting at work the next night and a friendly co-worker was giving away huge boxes of overly ripe bananas from a store she works at during the day. I was thrilled because I freeze sliced bananas for my vanilla soy-milk smoothies and here were bunches of them *for free*. I carried the heavy banana box to my car with a greedy grin like I had just won The Banana Lottery.

I also partook of free pizza at the staff meeting that night, the first time that a colleague has ever bought pizza for all fifty of us in the nine months I taught classes there.

Then Chris, the executor of the estate where I house sat, was in town and had fried up the last of my two eggs that morning for her breakfast while I was away, so later she thoughtfully replaced them with a full package of *eighteen.*

I was the grateful recipient of free food three times in one day.

So that took care of my food shortage, and I had delicious banana smoothies for months.

God cares about the littlest details when we do. I was still broke, in debt, and crazy around money, but God provided everything I needed right when I needed it.

FAMILY CONSTELLATION THERAPY

I was willing to try almost anything. I needed a friend to help me script the structured psychotherapy, so I asked my supportive friend, Renee, to role-play a family member for me. The family constellation therapist, Jamie, who lived in Minnesota, offered me a free phone session to help me remove my blocks to earning more money. Since I didn't have other people available on a workday to stand in for me, I brought sheets of copy paper to symbolize my absent family members.

Renee and I stood on the shore of pristine Lake Murray in La Mesa, California, on a sunlit morning with the sound of ducks and the faint smell of eucalyptus in the warm air. I called Jamie on my cell phone at the appointed time. I described the lakeside scene to her. Like actors in a play, Jamie asked me to have Renee play my dad. I had Renee stand on a wide tree stump, making her tall and powerful like my dad.

"Where are you standing?" she asked me, so she could get a visual layout.

"I'm standing about ten paces away, in front of him,

crouched on the ground near a trash can. I feel small and unworthy, like I always did around my dad," I said in a child's voice. Never mind that I was over fifty and two thousand miles away from him.

Jamie instructed, "Tell your dad, 'I am little and you're big.' Say it three times."

I said this out loud, feeling childish, and I was surprised to find myself crying. I felt so little again, ashamed, and powerless. I was shocked that I felt this way.

Jamie said, "Let me talk to Renee."

Renee took the phone from me, then held herself steady on the uneven stump, looking at me with her compassionate brown eyes.

"Try telling her, 'You're my daughter and I love you." Jamie instructed.

As if she were my father, Renee said it to me.

I sat there with my nose wrinkled, shaking my head from side to side in disbelief. After Renee described my reaction to her, Jamie told her to say it again.

"You are my daughter. I love you."

Why was it easier to believe that Renee was my dad than it was to believe that my dad loved me? In heaving pain now, I wanted the therapy to work, so I kept with it, even though it was increasingly uncomfortable.

Renee looked at me with sympathy.

"I hear the words," I said meekly, "but I don't believe you."

Jamie was on the phone with me again, "Try moving closer to your dad."

"I can't." I felt too fearful to move. I took out a piece of paper and placed it in the dirt in front of me, like a white fence. "I need a shield to feel safe." I insisted.

"OK," Jamie agreed.

Like a scared six-year-old who needed to hide, I laid that paper shield on the ground halfway between my towering father and me. There was a strange comfort having that barrier there for protection.

As instructed, I used another sheet of paper for my mom and one for my younger brother, Tim. Both papers were next to me in a lateral lineup, not too close to me, and about the same distance away from my dad. That felt like the right placement for all of us.

Renee looked flushed, standing rigidly in the sun on that sloping stump. I felt mean making her stand there in the heat, and rather ridiculous as I crouched down, teary-eyed behind a piece of paper on the ground, a curious spectacle for passing joggers.

"OK, it's done." I felt sad looking at the physical structure, symbolic of my original family.

"Is there someone missing?" Jamie asked.

"Huh?" A trained psychotherapist myself, I thought we were getting off track now. "Well, yes, but—"

"Who is missing?"

"My older half-sister, Lyn," I said, surprising myself. "But she was given up for adoption before I was born so I never met her." *How on Earth can this matter? I am terrified of my own dad, disbelieving he loves me, and now this is going in the wrong direction.* I felt vulnerable and horribly exposed in front of Renee, whose face looked confused and pinker from the heat.

"Put a piece of paper out there for your sister," Jamie told me.

I did as she said. I placed Lyn off to the left side several yards away, outside the nuclear family triangle. I told Jamie where Lyn's paper was placed.

"How does she feel out there all by herself?" Jamie asked me.

I had to think hard about this. How might it feel to be an older sister, raised alone, who was adopted as a baby?

My dad hadn't known she existed until ten years ago. A woman named Lyn had called him from Los Angeles, claimed to be his daughter, and asked if he would take a paternity test.

He traveled from Minnesota to see her in L.A. and the lab results were positive. They met again at my dad's house in Eden Prairie, Minnesota, and exchanged a few calls and e-mails, and that was it.

I found out that my dad was only fifteen years old when he got his girlfriend, Barb, also fifteen, pregnant. Barb's pregnancy was a secret, and the young girl was immediately whisked away to California to live with her aunt. My dad never saw or talked to his first love again.

Barb gave Lyn up for adoption to this same aunt, who raised Lyn as an only child. Until she was an adult, Lyn grew up believing that her aunt, who adopted her, was her mother.

I suddenly felt what it might be like to be Lyn when she found out the truth. She was adopted, away from her biological father, even her own mother, and then she learned about me and Tim, her younger half-siblings. She must have felt completely outcast. To me, it felt lonely and lousy. As Lyn, I wouldn't want to meet the entitled half-sister who was raised by my real dad. Was she disinterested, jealous, envious? She was definitely alienated from everyone.

"Ask Renee how she feels being your dad, and knowing about Lyn now."

Renee straightened up and balanced herself to take her dutiful role as my dad.

As him, she said, "I feel ashamed that I got her pregnant and the baby had to be adopted."

I understood. I empathized with my teen dad's shame and grief. It took me out of myself to think of him as a lonely high school boy, brokenhearted, not knowing what happened to his girlfriend or why they broke up. The mystery around her sudden disappearance from school must have been disturbing and hard for him.

"Put your sister in her right place in your family now." I heard Jamie say.

I took the distant white paper that symbolized Lyn and moved it into the eldest sibling position, directly in front of me, between me and my dad. When I did that, I didn't need to be shielded anymore. I brushed aside the obsolete paper barrier, and gently placed my big sister into her rightful spot as the oldest.

I was his middle child now.

This made me feel far less conspicuous. A ton of self-imposed pressure lifted. I wasn't the oldest daughter anymore. I didn't have to be The Star, the overachiever trying to be perfect. I didn't have to prove anything to anyone. I felt safe behind my older sister now, who could be the hero, my protector, the buffer between Dad and me.

"You are my daughter and I love you."

I heard it again and this time I *felt* it. It was true. He loved me. He loved my sister Lynn too–he loved us both. Things had shifted somehow, and I could trust the feeling. An awe-filled peace came over me, and I was moved and speechless, like a birth and a death had just taken place.

I stood close to Dad now, close enough to see the sweat beads on Renee's forehead. I wanted to move my trusted friend into the cool shade, to reward her for her helpful therapeutic work in this strange emotional scenario she was witnessing.

How bizarre that a sister I had never met was missing from my life, and yet my soul knew. She was alive, and then she was gone. Now, longing to have her in my life, I ached for her. It was like a burning, basic need.

Jamie told me to stand facing away from Dad, while he stood behind me holding his strong hands on my shoulders, uncharacteristic of him.

Then I heard Renee, who was prompted, say, "I'm here to support you now."

With Renee's comforting hands, and imagining Dad was there for me, I felt encouraged in a way I never had. I cried harder. I had my sister back in place, and now I had Dad, too. My heart was full of love for them. We all came together powerfully that day at the lake, like a symbolic spiritual reunion; with a sweaty Renee and a brilliant unseen family constellation therapist.

I was profoundly changed over the next few days. I couldn't talk about it. Who would believe me and how could I explain it? The experience felt too sacred. I was stunned and amazed that this unknown loss had affected me so deeply—that it was so essential to my identity. I had missed out on having a big sister my whole life and I grieved. In some insidious way, I had tried to make up for her absence, as if I could, by proving how worthy I was, when I never really had to. As the second daughter now, I relaxed. I could just be myself now, defects and all.

I tried to reach my sister Lyn a couple of times after

this. I left her brief voice mails about wanting to meet her if she would like to, but she hasn't called back. When I called Dad for Lyn's phone number, he said Lyn had been sick for over a month. It started about the time of the phone therapy. I didn't connect with her in person, that was her choice, but that day at the lake I somehow connected with her spiritually and emotionally.

Without revealing what happened in my therapy session, I phoned Dad and apologized for my wrongs in our estranged relationship, and thanks to Lyn, I found a new forgiveness with him that helped me heal.

MONEY AND THE BEGGAR

Jubilantly I said a resounding "Yes!" to my abundance, out loud, with my head lifted up to the sky-gods in gratitude for another incredible day in San Diego. I was roller-skating down the touristy Mission Beach Boardwalk on a glorious Saturday morning, after having said my prayers. I felt an enthusiastic receptivity for new good to come to me.

God must have known I was short on cash, because I found two twenty dollar bills on the sidewalk. I scooped them up on my skates without breaking my stride. Then I spun around to see who the cash might belong to. I noticed a man walking a few yards ahead of me with his hands in his pockets and thought maybe he had lost his cash.

I skated up to him. "Excuse me, Sir, did you lose some money?" I asked from behind him.

He turned around, looked startled. "Oh, did I?"

"I'm asking you—if you lost some money?" I stopped and made eye contact with him.

He reached into his pants pockets. "No."

There was no one else around to ask. The bills were

mine; divine sprinkles from heaven. *Thank you.* I smiled as I roller-skated away, like God's kid with a new allowance. I got my morning decaf at Woody's for two bucks, like I do every weekend, and sat at the beachside table, watching the surfers rolling in on the big waves. I sipped the creamy coffee and sniffed the breakfast aroma of fried onions and grilled peppers.

A gruff-looking homeless man in his sixties shuffled up to the innocent man eating eggs next to me and asked him for a nickel. The startled young man looked up and shook his head no. The homeless man, in a bulky winter coat that hadn't been to a Laundromat, suddenly became loud and belligerent.

"Go to hell then!" He yelled at the wide-eyed egg-gobbler.

I was next in line along the narrow bar table. I smiled with compassion into his heartsick, mentally ill eyes and said with respect, "I will give you three dollars if you will tell him you are sorry." After all, I was so abundantly blessed with cash now.

"I only asked for a *nickel*!" he purged, angrily spitting on me a little, as if the man's rejection of his coin request meant he was worth less than five cents.

"Well, I will give you three dollars. A nickel isn't enough. You need more than that."

I think he could tell I was serious, but he hesitated. Every man is worth far more than a nickel, even an unpredictable, malodorous one.

He growled under his alcoholic breath, but he lunged over to the insulted man and garbled out a quick apology, then slung-shot back at me for his reward.

I gave him the three dollars he had earned and smiled at him. "God bless you…" I stamped him with that idea as he left. When I feel blessed, I want to bless others.

I felt like I had been put back in my humble place when the beggar shouted up to the big blue sky, "*God* is God," then staggered away down the boardwalk, and vanished behind a bush.

TYRA AND THE FLOWER SHOP

Inpatient men were lined up to buy their sweethearts cut roses, a required Valentine's purchase for domestic harmony, to prevent holiday holdouts, and to by-step any babe backlash. It was the busiest day of the year at the floral shop. I worked as a temp to help my friend Peggy in Minnesota one year ago. I remember I wore my festive pink and red blouse to be in a romantic holiday mode as I joyfully served the male flack-avoiders.

This year I was back in San Diego and I decided to work another Valentine's Day. Marilyn, the pleasant owner of the California flower shop, hired me to temp there, and I was all set to go in to train for my first day. But there was a problem with me. I felt sick. I couldn't budge from my soft bed that morning. My legs wouldn't move. I didn't have any romance left in me. I felt nothing but pure dread and strong foreboding.

What is going on with me? Shoot, I told Marilyn I would work. My word is important to me . . . but I don't want to go.

Then it hit me like a flat volleyball. I had been so

pathetically in love with Dave last year. He had ordered a luxurious Valentine bouquet for me, one that my floral designer co-workers made extra special just for me. Dave called them and told them to make it outstanding, so they secretly studied my comments throughout the workday as I "oohed" and "ahhhed" over certain exotic flowers and the scents I liked best.

"Oh, I love these hot pink and giant red roses!" I exclaimed as I carried them to the cooler with my nose buried in them. My colleagues looked at each other, winked, and smirked. Then I would praise the regal Stargazer lilies, the fragrant white freesias, and my filler of choice, pink wax flower. I didn't know they were in cahoots, all eavesdropping.

As I was about to leave the shop for the evening, I was presented with a giant custom bouquet they were all in on. I was teary-eyed and so grateful to have a man who cared that much, and a group of floral artists who made it a special event.

"He even called to make sure you got it," Peggy stood proudly.

Wow, my heart was full.

But this year, without Dave, everything felt wrong.

All I recalled now were the thorn-shaped cuts burning my fingertips, the low pay, and the incredible stress. Perhaps the grief of losing Dave was again calling the shots. I fought with myself, and then decided to take care of myself foremost. I had to call Marilyn to tell her I just couldn't work.

I dialed the florist number and as I made the cell phone connection, I heard them dialing out too, at the same time.

"Carolyn?" Marilyn, who I was calling, asked me first.

"Yes?" I said, bewildered. *Who is calling who?*

"Park elsewhere," she commanded. "Our parking lot is full. Park at Vons."

I heard park elsewhere, and thought, *precisely! That is exactly my intent.*

"I decided to go with another opportunity," I said, trying to sound confident and businesslike, rather than the weakling I was, wiggling out of work.

"Oh, OK." She sounded disappointed.

We hung up and instant relief descended upon me, tinged with a bit of guilt for bailing out at the last minute.

I went to my women's lunch meeting the next day

feeling depressed about no Dave, no flowers, no one to share Valentine's Day with, and now no part-time income either. *Should I have worked?* I hate those indecisive moments when I question something I've already done.

A thirty year-old attractive gal named Tyra, who I was remotely acquainted with but had never talked to before, approached me to chat.

I told her I had opted out of the florist assistant role and she told me that she had worked at that *exact same flower shop* on Valentine's Day the year before, for five dollars *less* an hour than I had agreed to work for.

"It was horrible." She scrunched up her pretty face. "It was so busy and stressful that it took me a week to recover from the exhaustion afterwards."

Wow, God must've been listening to me again, because after she said that, I knew I had definitely done the right thing. Thanks Tyra. Thanks God, for making that connection.

CROWS AND ROSES

There was more junk and clutter in the garage where I house-sat than you could imagine. It was my job to clear it out. I saw a damaged half-bag of ancient weed killer-lawn fertilizer and rather than throwing it into the trash can, I decided the lawn needed greening. I spread it over the front lawn with a cup like salting a steak. I scattered the granules until the old bag was empty. I was pleased I used it all up to benefit the neglected grass—until the next day.

I noticed an unpleasant chemical smell as I passed the front yard to get to my car in the driveway. It overpowered the sweet fragrance of the front rose bed that I had enjoyed a day earlier. Then I noticed the hungry black crows fervently pecking away at the newly fertilized grass, the toxic granules being lifted into their tiny beaks, and a feeling of doom engulfed me.

Am I poisoning them?

I should have thrown that awful stuff away. Now the neighborhood wildlife is going to eat it, get sick, maybe even die, and it will be my thoughtlessness that did it. I felt concerned, but I got in my car and drove off to meet some friends for lunch.

I had been fertilizing the front roses, too, with cut-up banana peels, great advice from my aunt Diane. She said they really liked the potassium. I could see they were blooming more profusely after I had spread the blackening peels around. It was easy to cut up bunches of bananas to freeze slices for my smoothies, and then use the discards to feed the hungry roses. It felt like the right and natural thing to do, and being organic appealed to me.

* * *

A few days after the ravenous crows ate the tasty lawn fertilizer, I clipped a few bursting rosebuds and placed the stems in a glass vase with water to take to a friend. I had driven a few miles with the vase in a small box on the floor of my car when I had to slam on the brakes in the restaurant parking lot.

A vicious crow fight had ensued outside the front of my car. I was stunned. It looked like they were in a battle to the death. That's how intense it was.

My gut alarm went off as a disoriented crow, the one getting the worst of the beating, flapped its wings haphazardly, then tumbled and smashed into the front of my bumper. I stopped instantly, but my rose vase spilled its water all over the carpeted floor mat.

"Darn it!" I wanted that vase of flowers for my friend. Were these the same crows from my yard? Were they furious from being poisoned and lashing out at each other in pain? Their scuffle even affected the cut roses I had grown organically.

Was there a sign in all of this for me?

I learned my lesson to stop using toxic chemicals that day, to start using my brain on how these unconscious actions are going to affect the animals, plants, the soil, and our future generations that will be living on this planet long after I'm gone.

What we do has subtle or not so subtle long-term effects, but most of us never pay attention to cause and effect.

My little karma-crow gave me the message clearly. That day I felt like the universe was showing me that I needed to be more careful and most of all, be true to my values, and true to myself.

HOW I BECAME A PROFESSIONAL SINGER

Well-intentioned family members cautioned me, "It's hard to make it as a singer," "There's a lot of competition out there," and, "You're a good singer, Carolyn, but you're not a *great* singer." Undaunted, I set out to prove that I was, with God's help, some kind of singer anyway.

It took a lot of *overcoming* to be a professional soloist—working through personal inadequacies, my fear of straining my tender voice box, of running out of breath, and the universal fear of embarrassing myself in public. As I practiced and became more confident, my sureness grew, and I felt that I was meant to sing, uplift, and inspire others with music.

The idea to sing in senior centers came to me when I worked as a Licensed Social Worker at a long-term care facility. I heard a painfully loud *awf*-key singer crooning like he was full of himself. Those poor residents, I thought, how can they stand that noise? Certainly, some of them were hard of hearing, but this was ridiculous.

Geez, even I *can do better than that!*

* * *

So I practiced—a lot. My greatest talent-developing tool was my tape recorder. I sang a song, recorded it, played it back and then picked it apart. Ouch, that key was off, or ooh, that was a little weak in that spot. Then I would sing it again, and again, and again—until I liked it. It was like falling in the water with wind surfing—I just had to keep getting back on board with a better approach until it worked. If I liked it, then maybe somebody else would too.

When they say the show must go on, what does that mean? For me it meant showing up despite waves of nausea, diarrhea, and bad hair—all felt equally fatal. It meant squelching my own personal emotions, despite a family death or big disappointment, or a stubborn case of a lazy "I don't want to." I always managed to pull it off somehow, no matter what, and start on time.

They don't give standing ovations to so-so singers, or so I'm told. At one repeat performance, I walked in to find the same group of seniors I had performed for a month earlier, all remembering me. I watched awestruck as they stood up, clapped, and cheered for me as I merely rolled in with my sound equipment!

Huh? I haven't even started to sing yet. Is this really for me? Teary-eyed and grateful, I knew I had actually *earned* this honor. All that tedious vocal practice paid off.

There is so much to think about while I'm performing—the timing of the music, my dance moves, the lyrics, appropriate facial expressions, not tripping over the mike cord, connecting with the audience, thus all the other extraneous details, like my appearance, must be dealt with prior to the performance.

Besides my sound check, I always peered at my teeth in the mirror before a gig for my "broccoli check." I learned not to wear any funky clothes you have to fuss with or worry about. No zippers that drop while you're dancing, no too-big tights that droop when you wiggle, and most of all, my fancy dresses had to hide sweaty armpits and belly bulges. Imagining my big debut someday, I looked at the sparkly floor-length gown hanging in my closet for a year before I wore it on stage.

While entertaining an audience, I ignored the trespassing waiters, wailing wheel chair alarms that tattle on elders who try to stand up on their own, the unescorted Alzheimer's patients who dance inches from my face with sour breath. They can't remember what they had for lunch—or even if they had lunch yet, but they howl-sing like banshees to the song, "You Are My Sunshine."

I still remember most of the words to tunes I learned as a kid, too.

I was eleven years old when we had "concerts" in our big basement in Bloomington, Minnesota. Our so-called band, The Colony Five, consisted of me, the producer and director, my compliant younger brother Timmy, my best friend Janine, and her siblings, Paula and Ronnie. We sang (more like lip-synched) our love songs to Donny Osmond and Michael Jackson songs with choreographed dance moves to thrill the neighbor kids we babysat for. We even made enough money from the tickets (and snack bar) to buy new jean jackets. Now that was success!

So I was an entrepreneur and singer at age eleven. I think Danny Thomas said it best, "It only takes twenty years to become an overnight success." He never mentioned how many different bands most singers have to go through. None ever meant more than The Colony Five.

My ex-husband, Howard, a disc jockey, is credited for pulling me out on stage to sing "Happy Birthday" to an auditorium full of teenagers. I didn't die from terror, I loved performing, and I started booking paid gigs.

Our big professional debut was all set with two friends I met roller-skating; Lori, a soprano, and Kathie, my harmony buddy. I sang the lead melody. Our trio, The Dazzling W's (because all of our last names began with a W—how clever) performed at Home Cookin' Café, a mediocre diner that catered to crusty old truckers. We thought that fifty dollars each and a choice of any steak dinner afterwards was fantastic. We set up the karaoke music equipment and were ready to croon when our soprano suddenly got the jitters.

"There's a man smoking over there," Lori wailed, a little too passionately.

I was irritated by the smoker too, but I wasn't going to make a big deal out of it. She, on the other hand, was.

Lori insisted, "I can't sing with that smoke."

I watched horrified as Lori ran out of the restaurant! This was serious. We had practiced as a trio for several months, perfecting our three part harmonies for this show. It was a freezing winter night and I had driven all of us to the café. She fled into the night in the bitter cold on foot. I looked outside. She was gone.

Kathie and I looked at each other in terror. *What do we do now?* We quickly reassembled ourselves as a duet. We sang together and they loved us. We got tips, we got applause, we got propositioned, and we got juicy porterhouse steaks with desserts. Lori's big debut was thwarted by her fear, but The Dazzling W's duo was born! That gig continued once a month, then once every two weeks, then weekly on Saturday nights until every booth was packed full, and they weren't our relatives anymore.

When I moved to San Diego in 2002, I went solo. As of 2014, I've performed 700 shows that I booked at hundreds of senior centers. I've been to some low-end, depressing nursing homes, and the most upscale retirement centers you can imagine—with illuminated entryway fountains, elaborate flower gardens, chandeliers, and rich, burgundy carpets.

I've jiggled to "Lets Twist Again," did drum-beat high kicks to "Johnny Be Goode," and got the audience singing along to "Que Sera Sera." I even saw a toothless senior smile while playing my cow bell. I've sung "Happy Birthday" to centenarians, and watched wheelchair-bound elders dance like whirlwinds.

The secret to my success is this: I prayed before

every performance, "Please God, make me an instrument of your love, your strength, your peace, and your joy." At one church service I prayed to God, "Please let me touch their hearts." After that show a woman came up to me, in tears and clutching her chest and said, "You really touched my heart." *Wow*.

Intuitive Marjorie Klemp, the revered former wife of the spiritual leader of Eckankar, approached me after my song once and said, "You sing to their souls…"

Yes, that's what I do.

It was well worth all the years of hard work it took. So many people want instant success, but I've learned that true success is *earned*. It is fought for. It may be a long struggle and yet the rewards do come. The standing ovations are real because the audience seems to understand what had to be overcome, what inner and outer challenges had to be endured in order to share this once raw, and now polished, gift. With their love, I found my voice and a true passion.

I still may not be a great singer, but I'm having a great time!

THE U.P.S. GUY

My music amplifier died.

I had a singing engagement coming up so I ordered a new amp on EBay. They promised delivery on Tuesday. I was at my day job so I missed the UPS delivery truck the first day, but I saw their sticky note on my door, saying they would be back the next day, and needed my signature. I signed it and stuck it back on the door. I had to have it by Thursday. One of my favorite clients hired me to sing for a big holiday dance.

I just had to have that amp!

Wednesday I came home from work expecting to see a big box at my door (C'mon Santa) but nope, just another sticky note. It said, "Sender requires a signature." The one I had signed was still dangling. *Hadn't they seen it?* If I wasn't nervous enough about not having my amp yet, then I had to leave for a dreaded dentist appointment.

The next day, Thursday, my mouth felt like it had been jackhammered, so I stayed home from work with a headache. Still no amp, and a big gig to do that night, I called the UPS number.

"Where's my shipment?" I asked.

I heard: "We can't guarantee a time or reach the driver. We need a signature in person. It will be delivered between now and seven pm."

"But I have to leave for my show at four." I felt myself start to get worried. Refusing to think the worst, I told the man, "All right then, I will just pray that he gets here by four, and I do believe that he will." I hung up and put my faith to work and prayed with my entire soul, believing my words.

Please God, I need that amp. I need it here before I leave for my show at four o'clock. I know you can do it. I believe it will be here. I have faith in you. And so it is.

I went about my business for the day at home, envisioning my amp coming in time, knowing it would. I read my library books and watched old DVD's to distract me from my gum pain. At least my clean teeth would be white when I sang! The uneventful afternoon crept on.

At 3:30 I put everything I needed into my car, put on my red Christmas dress and did my makeup. At 3:59 my music equipment was loaded and I had to go.

Still no amp.

I confirmed my faith. I told God, "I know you will

bring my amp." I had on my coat and heels. I was ready to leave the house when I heard the UPS truck coming. I ran outside laughing euphorically, opened my trunk, and asked the timely UPS guy to please put it right in there.

"I've been praying for this all day. Thank you so much." Giddy with God, I signed his electronic pad and shut the trunk door with my new amplifier in its box. I smiled at the UPS guy—he smiled back. I was thrilled.

It was 4:01 pm when I backed out of my driveway. My faith in God was rewarded. Cheering and thanking God, I drove intoxicated with joy all the way to my show.

UNWRITTEN LESSONS

They don't want to be here. In fact, they'd rather be just about anywhere *else*. They are court-ordered to attend my classes as a program requirement for driving under the influence (DUI), un-affectionately known as "Dewey."

Having been arrested for drunk driving, they come to class angry or ashamed with heads hanging, perhaps expecting to be punished, or beheaded, like waiting criminals. But it's just an adult education class to raise their awareness about alcohol and high-risk behaviors. They take six weekly class sessions and that's supposed to change their behavior and prevent them from driving drunk again. I hope so.

I had no intention of ever teaching DUI classes with my counseling skills, but a psychic told me I'd be teaching at the university level when I got to California. And here it is, manifesting as thirty students looking up at me at the podium. The warm fluorescent lights flicker a little over my head. The full classroom smells like dry-erase marker, stale cigarettes, and janitorial soap.

I call out the students first names to take attendance

like I do every day. They only see me once a week—for six weeks. But I see different students every day, five days a week, every week. I look up from my Tuesday roster and make that first important eye contact with my new students. At that pivotal second, I send out a glance of genuine compassion, a look of high regard for that individual, a unique soul now entrusted in my care. I nod with respect to each one.

Somehow this small act disarms even the most belligerent involuntary client.

They've all been jailed briefly for violating the drunk-driving law so I tell my silly joke. "What do you call a midget psychic who escaped from jail?" I smile, looking at their eager faces. "A small medium at large!"

They seem to snicker more from my intended effort than the punch line.

Equipped with my master's degree in counseling psychology and a two-year certificate in alcohol and other drug studies, I teach them about the dangers of drinking and driving, and what it means to abuse alcohol from the perspective of a counselor who has worked in several rehabs. Sometimes I share my own personal story if I think it might benefit my students.

"I got a DUI in Minnesota in 1982," I said, "and I thought I was so unfortunate, being court-ordered to attend an alcohol treatment program, but I ended up being the lucky one. I stayed free of alcohol after that wake-up call. The other two people who were with me the night I got arrested didn't fare as well. Bob, who was in my car when I got the DUI, continued to drink alcohol and smoke marijuana, and he died of throat cancer at the age of forty-two. My other passenger, a woman-friend, became an alcoholic, married an alcoholic, and had two little boys with developmental disabilities. Alcohol ingested during pregnancy is the number one cause of mental retardation in our country."

Now I really have their attention. It's not me versus them, it's *us*.

Suddenly the students jump, startled, as a dazed black bird outside bashes its head into the large classroom window, flying into it not once, but three times.

"That, ladies and gentleman, is insanity," I say, "doing the same thing over and over and expecting different results." Even that crazy bird, like everything that happens in class, is an educational moment. It's all about shifting harmful attitudes and actions. This class is a rather mild consequence for their extremely poor judgment.

The messy-haired elderly man I just met, Hank, with bloodshot, shame-filled eyes, who shared with me before class that he is here for his *seventh* DUI, suddenly gets up from his seat and goes to sit in the corner.

Somehow, that seems more appropriate.

"Let's go around the room and introduce ourselves," I say cheerfully from the white board at the front, where I have written my name for them and these three questions:

1. Your Name

2. A Class Rule (with a smiley face next to it and two eyes in the shape of plus signs so they appear positive.)

3. Your favorite vegetable and how you like it prepared.

That last one is just for fun—an icebreaker. It's always better when the rules are stated out loud by the students themselves, so they take responsibility for them, and I'm not the despised dictator or wicked warden. I try to make it amusing to recite the rules no one wants to hear.

"How do we say the rules in class?" I ask the students who have been here before, so the newcomers will know how we do things.

"Positively," they chime in together, united with knowledge from previous classes.

"And how do we do that?" I smile, looking at their faces for answers.

"By omitting the words 'no, don't, can't, mustn't and *shan't!*'" They recite what they have been told before. No one says shan't for shouldn't anymore. That's why I say it. They seem to like it by the laughter I hear and see.

The new students look perplexed. Some appear bored. A few are amused, as evidenced by their half-smiles, but most seem unaffected. Apathy is a common facial expression . . . at first.

"We can change our self-talk by changing our negative thoughts to positive ones. Instead of saying, '*Don't run* down the hall, we say, '*Please walk* down the hall.' A few eyes roll, but most of them are with me. "Can you feel how it changes the energy in the room?"

They nod yes.

I am empathetic. I feel their emotional energy, and often see their aura energy above their heads too.

I read the *indigo* auras of my exceptional students most readily, because they are generally the most enlightened. But they still need to learn about DUI prevention and greater personal safety skills.

Question number three asks them about their *favorite vegetable* and gets them thinking about their nutritional needs, even learning new recipes from each other, but it mainly gets them to tune-in to the long list of facility rules that seem like dreaded detention.

Each student introduces himself—by first name only—to protect confidentiality. They each voice one class rule; silencing their cell phones, wearing appropriate clothing (like no beer ads on shirts), respecting each other in class and so on. When they slip up and say, "Don't be late," I gently urge them to rephrase it more positively.

"Please be on time," an older student pipes in, wearing a bulging white muscle shirt. He corrects himself quickly as he pulls on his friend's gray hooded sweatshirt to cover his marijuana tattoo. Shirts must have sleeves. That's the rule.

Finally, after everyone has had their turn stating their name, a class rule, and their favorite veggie, steamed broccoli and grilled asparagus win the popularity contest.

"So why are we talking about *vegetables* in a DUI program? What's the big deal?" I say with a smile as I search their faces for answers, scanning all three rows of ten students across.

Some look inquisitive, others smile, a few look sleepy, a big man burps.

"When we eat raw vegetables," I claim, "we heal our brains that may have been damaged by toxic alcohol and drugs. Vegetables and fruits help heal our brain cells with nutrition."

They appear unmoved.

"And on the other hand, if one continues on the progressive road to addiction and alcoholism, one may experience a wet brain, go into a coma, or become an accidental quadriplegic, or in politically incorrect terms, *become a vegetable*."

I hear groans. I see some wrinkled noses and several smirks. They appear to get it.

Abruptly, a cell phone rings and the guilty party gets up and leaves the classroom unprompted, knowing he has just been disqualified from his seat. He will have to make up the class and pay twenty five dollars for his oversight. There is no leeway on this. We are all bound by the laws of the land.

The class numbers themselves off, from one to four. They break up into four small groups of seven or eight.

Then they go to their whiteboards and write questions and answers posed to them, such as, "What myths have you heard that claim to make a person sober?" They dispel the myth that says coffee can make you sober, when it only creates a nervous, wide-awake drunk. And a penny under your tongue won't beat the breath-analyzer test, ever.

Each group has an elected leader who speaks on behalf of their small group, reading off the written answers they listed as a team. They enjoy this. I take a casual back seat to the learning process. Adept public speakers suddenly spring forth from each group. Once their presentations are complete, I make comments of my own and then I always make sure I praise their efforts.

"Your boards look fabulous and your answers are very thorough." I gush over them and beam. They beam back. I hope it overrides some of the shame and guilt many of them feel about being here. When they finish their board exercise, I start my little lecture.

"What is the *one* thing that will make you sober?" I ask, because it's on the quiz.

"Time," they say in unison.

Time is a four-letter word for the students who ran for that "last call" at bar closing time. They spiked their body's blood-alcohol level just before they drove home. I tell each group that a responsible drinker will have a designated driver, a cab, or wait it out for a few hours. They didn't do that. They drove drunk and ended up here, lucky to be alive. There are worse things than getting a DUI or going to jail. They could have injured or killed someone. There are tens of thousands of drunk-driving deaths every year on American highways.

They could have been one of them.

I show a snazzy 1970s video of all the horrible things alcohol, a natural poison, does to the body. Then we view tragic preventable car accidents that affect far too many people. I end the class by telling them how what they do matters—for good or ill—and how they affect people with their actions and attitudes. I have never seen so many faces light up as when I remind them that they have a lot of personal power; that what they do matters.

I care about them and I think they sense it. I didn't like their profanity, or the smell of smoke after their break. I didn't cherish the negative attitudes some of them flaunted early on. But I cared for them all as precious human beings, awakening souls, as much as a doting grandmother goose reins in her favored flock, protecting them from nearby predators.

Sometimes the enemy is their own unexamined behavior and destructive habits.

Did they learn anything from me?

If nothing else, they surely learned to speak more positively by omitting the words no, don't, can't, and shan't. They learned that they have the power to affect everyone around them with their actions, that they can change their negative thoughts, and they have a choice to be a radiating force for sobriety and recovery, a responsible drinker, or a drunk who hurts people. They each cause ripples in life just as surely as a stone dropped into a pond. *They matter.*

After they graduate from the corny canned presentations that I'm required to teach, the unwritten lessons were probably the most important things they learned. By exam day, they hold their heads a little higher.

Class is dismissed. They file out, shaking my hand, thanking me for teaching them to take care of themselves.

"This was the best DUI class I've had!"

I look up to see a gleam in the eyes of the grinning guy with the seven DUIs.

What a Life!

I flew to Jamaica alone for a stay

To windsurf a stretch of Montego Bay

Moon-danced on a patio in Cancun

And went up in the sky in a hot-air balloon

I've roller-skated in the San Diego sun

And danced in flash mobs just for fun

I sailed the Bahamas on a honeymoon cruise

Got paid to sing songs like "Blue Suede Shoes"

I've boogie boarded on waves in the sea

Many beaus have been in pursuit of me

I've packed up my life to start it all over

With just a backpack of dreams on my shoulder

I graduated college in the top six percent

Then made lots of money but don't know where it went

I restored an old house into a nice home for me

I even gave a speech in Washington D.C.

I hung out at the Hilton on Mission Bay

Watching sparkles on the water on a sunshiny day

I walked the same beaches where presidents stood

And accomplished things I never thought I could

I've sung with an excellent band on a stage

I walked out on jobs when they felt like a cage

I've been to the desert and lived by the beach

And worked at a school where they paid me to teach

I've skied down a mountain at break neck speed

Gave up drinking and smoking weed

Jogged along the shoreline collecting shells

Sung in the world's most upscale hotels

I've counseled hundreds of adults and teens

Written published pieces in magazines

Sung to audiences that stood and cheered

Faced many things that I formerly feared

In many ways I've lived the life of my dreams

More of a soloist than a member of teams

And it all simmers down to what it's all of

Just being a part of the world in God's love.

THE TREASURE CHEST

After what seemed like endless financial failures, one day I earnestly asked God, "How do I connect to my abundance?" Then I went into deep meditation. In my mind's eye I saw an old pirate's treasure chest floating on the open sea, bobbing up and down on the current as it made its way to me. I opened it and it was full of gold coins. Then I heard a mighty voice say, "You have already earned it. Here it is—it is yours . . ."

What? I already earned it, but how?

I realized that the closest thing I had to a treasure chest was an old brown trunk that held all my diaries, musty old journals that kept the secrets of my life private and tucked away. I saved them for that far-off day when I was confined to a nice rocking chair in some quaint little nursing home, with time to read my memoirs.

Then it occurred to me that maybe this was what was meant to unfold. Perhaps I had to be poor before I could appreciate my success. I also had to trust and rely on God for everything. Maybe I needed to be unemployed so I could write my book for a year.

All my life I'd been trying to be like everybody else—to fit in and do what they did to make money. I had been trying to live from the outside in. I had it all wrong. God wants me to live from the inside out. *My* insides. Singing is like that for me, a joyful passion, but it hasn't supported me fully. Being of service and helping people was what I always liked doing. Writing was something I enjoyed. Yet it never occurred to me to be an author.

Could I really just be myself? Do work I love? Share my take on the world? Publish my book of true stories?

This single mom who worked her way through college, who always felt like an outsider, suddenly opened wide, surrendering to God's will. Where once I felt like I didn't belong here or anywhere, now I knew I really belonged *everywhere.* I had a purpose all along.

Was my futile job search for fourteen months in vain because I was supposed to write a book? Is that why I had a free house full of provisions? So I would have a sanctuary to write short stories about all my miracles and serendipity? Was I meant to discover my gift and share it?

I remembered working at a group home once because it was the only job I could find quickly in San Diego, and I liked mentoring at-risk kids.

An intuitive foster boy declared on my childcare shift, "You're an imposter."

That's precisely how my seventy-some jobs felt to me, like I was posing. Me trying to be someone else to fit into this mundane world, when I preferred to work at the creative endeavors I came up with, creating something out of nothing—but ideas.

Could I simply be myself now, a unique artist, a bold unicorn with my own protruding third eye charging into the unknown ether? Was it all right to finally burst out with my own written voice after singing everybody else's songs my whole life?

Could I really risk it, be open, vulnerable, and real? Set aside any self-centered fear, and put myself out there?

I envisioned a day when my book would be published and I would talk freely with my readers about the spiritual experiences we are all having. That would be my bliss, to connect with others on our spiritual paths.

I am eager to keep manifesting my desires and living new stories. Now multiply this by seven billion. Imagine how many life stories there are, when we listen.

* * *

THE BUZZ

Listening deeply to the silence
As I lay in this warm bed
Clearing all the day's debris
That cluttered up my head

My body overrides my mental muses
With a dirge of noisy digestive juices
Jonesin' for a gelato, I hear a feisty breeze
Commuters, aircraft, acorns fall from trees

A hummingbird's song and a sparrow's trill
A Harley revving up a far-off hill
A cawing crow from the top branch, being king
The insecure Chihuahua that barks at everything

Vibrating, my breath, my aliveness shone
With billions of others, I lie here alone
Part of the humming buzz of the cosmos
The universal drone.

FLOAT

How I love to float and fly
Looking down from way up high
Chasing moonbeams in the sky
That little flash of light is I

How I love to swoop and float
And sail the seas without a boat
And swim beneath the waves so fair
Without ever coming up for air

As soul I can do most anything
And greater deeds than these
I can turn into a beam of light
Converging with the breeze

I can place my light inside of you
And feel the things you feel
You may say, "Oh yeah? Dream on..."
But our dreams are just as real

Sliding barefoot on roofs in the rain
Gliding along on a trackless train
Bouncing off hillsides without a care
Adventures of being spiritually aware.

ABOUT THE AUTHOR

Carolyn Jaynes' first article appeared in *The Minneapolis Star Tribune* when she was sixteen. She has kept a diary since age twelve, and her book is based on her journal entries. Carolyn earned her master's degree in counseling psychology, and has entertained thousands as a professional singer. A former alcohol and drug counselor, Carolyn realized she could uplift, inform, and inspire more people with her writing. Carolyn Jaynes lives in San Diego, California where she roller-skates at the beach, flirts with hummingbirds, and grows cucumbers.

CPSIA information can be obtained at www.ICGtesting.com
Printed in the USA
LVOW04s1924260515

439951LV00033B/1721/P

9 780991 477609